Pinocchio

THE ITALIAN LIST

GIORGIO AGAMBEN

Pinocchio

The Adventures of a Puppet,
Doubly Commented Upon and Triply Illustrated

TRANSLATED BY ADAM KOTSKO

LONDON NEW YORK CALCUTTA

THE ITALIAN LIST
Series Editor: Alberto Toscano

This book has been translated thanks to a translation grant awarded by the
Italian Ministry of Foreign Affairs and International Cooperation.

Questo libro è stato tradotto grazie a un contributo alla traduzione
assegnato dal Ministero degli Affari Esteri e della Cooperazione
Internazionale italiano.

Seagull Books, 2023

Originally published in Italian as Giorgio Agamben,
Pinocchio: *Le avventure di un burattino doppiamente commentate e tre volte illustrate*
© 2021 Giulio Einaudi editore s.p.a., Torino

First published in English translation by Seagull Books, 2023
English translation © Adam Kotsko, 2023

ISBN   978 1 80309 1 389

British Library Cataloguing-in-Publication Data
A catalogue record for this book is available from the British Library

Typeset at Seagull Books, Calcutta, India
Printed and bound by Hyam Enterprises, Calcutta, India

Contents

Translator's Note and Acknowledgments

Giorgio Agamben's original text uses an idiosyncratic reference system that dispenses with in-text references in favour of a series of 'bibliographical notes' at the end of the text, which contain a mixture of simple citations and more substantive comments. In order to bring this translation more in line with the norms of anglophone academia without losing any of the additional information provided in the original notes, I have opted to split the difference. I have added standard in-text references and an alphabetical list of works cited, while converting the most substantive comments into footnotes, among which I have also inserted some translator's notes.

For texts with no translation listed, all translations are my own; all other quoted translations are frequently altered for greater conformity with Agamben's interpretation and emphasis. For premodern texts available in many editions, standard textual divisions have been cited rather than page numbers. For in-text references with no page number given, either no page numbers exist (as with online news articles) or I was only able to find electronic editions that do not include page numbers. For the reader's convenience, I have also modernized the spelling, punctuation and (except when Agamben cites the full, lengthy subtitle) capitalization in quotations from Robert Kirk's *Secret Commonwealth*. All biblical quotations are based on the New Revised Standard Version.

Given the large number of editions of *The Adventures of Pinocchio*, both in Italian and in English translation, I have given chapter numbers rather than page numbers. To avoid unnecessary repetition of parenthetical citations, I have only marked the last reference in any given block of quotations from the same chapter before the sequence is interrupted by either a paragraph break or a quotation from another chapter or another work. In my quotations from that text, I have frequently revised existing translations to fit better with the context of Agamben's argument. Most often I have split the difference between Ann Lawson Lucas' 1996 translation (Collodi 2009a) and Nicolas J. Perella's 1986 translation (Collodi 1986) of the *The Adventures of Pinocchio*, while occasionally also consulting Geoffrey Brock's 2009 translation

(Collodi 2009b). Readers may also find it helpful to note that Agamben refers continually to the commentary of Giorgio Manganelli and often designates the author—whether ironically, affectionately, or both—as 'the glossator' or 'the commentator', frequently adding the adjective 'parallel' before either designation.

An important terminological distinction in the text is between *fiaba* and *favola*, which I have normally translated as 'fairy tale' and 'fable', respectively. The distinction between the two terms is, however, less clear than in English, and hence there are a couple places where I have translated *fiaba* as 'fable', with the author's permission. The adjective form *fiabesco* I have translated as 'fairy', 'fairy-tale' or 'fantastic', depending on the context. In the case of the term *picaro*, which derives from the Spanish *pícaro* but has been adopted as an Italian word, I have chosen to translate it back into Spanish. I have not sought any consistency in translating the various synonyms for 'ass' or 'donkey', though due to the more common vulgar usage of the former term, I have tended to limit its use to contexts related directly to Apuleius' *Golden Ass* or the Eleusinian mysteries.

I would like to thank Carlo Salzani for checking my translation and saving me from any number of errors, as well as helping me find several bibliographical references. I would also like to thank Alberto Toscano, Naveen Kishore, Bishan Samaddar, Sayoni Ghosh, Diven Nagpal and the entire editorial team at Seagull Books.

Adam Kotsko

Pinocchio

By God, I'm an ass who bears mysteries,
but I'm not going to bear them any further!
—Aristophanes, *Frogs*

And whoever laughs best today also laughs last.
—Nietzsche, *Twilight of the Idols*

Celestial (or Infernal?) Prologue

In the Bemporad edition illustrated by Carlo Chiostri that I have before my eyes (Collodi 1911), the sixth chapter of *Pinocchio* begins with these fateful words: 'As it happened, it was a terrible, hellish night.' Giorgio Manganelli, in his parallel commentary, says that instead, in 'two of the three texts [he has] used', it reads: 'It was a terrible winter [*d'inverno*] night' and draws from this the consequence that the reading 'hellish [*d'inferno*]' was a misprint 'both easy and difficult to recognize'. 'The original reading,' he incautiously adds, 'contains a wealth of information; among other things, it gives us the season of Pinocchio's birth' (Manganelli 2002: 40).

I do not know if critical editions of the codex of the marvellous puppet exist,[1] but a careful perusal of the texts that I have ready to hand seems to confirm the reading 'hellish [*d'inferno*]'. The bound copy collecting all of the issues

---

1 A critical edition of the book does in fact exist—see Collodi (1983).

published in 1881 of the *Giornale per i bambini* [Newspaper for children], in which 'the story of the puppet' was published for the first time, reads without a shadow of a doubt (from the sixth chapter, published in the 5th issue of 1881, p. 66—dated 4 August, thus at the height of summer; the first instalment had gone out 7 July): 'As it happened, it was a terrible, hellish [*d'inferno*] night,' and this reading, certainly less obvious, is thus philologically to be preferred to the *facilior* 'winter [*d'inverno*]'.

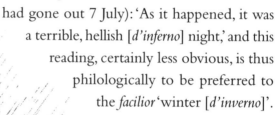

If this is the original reading, we do not know Pinocchio's birth date, but we do know where it took place: in hell [*all'inferno*]. The month is presumably—but not certainly—a winter one [*invernale*], since it is snowing ('Once the snow had stopped falling', we read when Pinocchio leaves the house with the alphabet book under his arm; chap. 9), but the season is in hell. After all, the wise commentator, who has just sacrificed philology to the desire to register a birth date, without delay connects 'the infernal misprint' with the flames that threaten the wooden puppet: since he comes from a 'forest', 'he has in common with plants the fear of an insidious danger by turns sudden and insinuating: fire' (Manganelli 2002: 42). It is the infernal element par excellence, but the glossator—who knows very well that 'what is essential and fateful in what happens to Pinocchio [. . .] happens in darkness' (54) and who, eight years later, published an unparalleled treatise on hell (Manganelli 2014b)—does not make the connection, at least for now, with Hades.

Manganelli cannot be ignorant of the fact that the real misprint is 'winter [*d'inverno*]'. It is he himself who observes that Pinocchio, when he recounts to Geppetto what has happened, uses precisely the same expression as the supposed blunder: ' "It was a terrible, hellish [*d'inferno*] night" (chap. 7), Pinocchio begins precipitously, with a phrase that explains and confirms the preceding misprint (or perhaps has the same possibility of being a misprint)' (Manganelli 2002: 48). Even if he had been completely ignorant [*profano*] of philology—but there is no sphere in which Manganelli's mind can be called ignorant [*profano*]—he certainly could not misunderstand the obvious, namely that Pinocchio's phrase, in 'repeating' the misprint, only proved that it is not one.

There must therefore be a reason why the parallel book wants at all costs to insert into the text a misprint, to read 'winter [*d'inverno*]' where 'hellish [*d'inferno*]' is written. And it is quickly found, as soon as one observes the care and caution with which Manganelli avoids every esoteric interpretation of the puppet's story. 'Winter' is a date on the calendar, 'hell' is laden with symbolic meanings and possible allegories.

The example par excellence of an esoteric reading is to be found in Elémire Zolla, according to whom Collodi's book bears witness to 'an almost intolerable esoteric profundity', whose origins are to be sought 'in the culture of the Masonic circles to which Collodi belonged'.[2] The book is the story of an initiation, the blue-haired Fairy is, obviously, Isis, 'the great mediatrix, representing the entire animal world or, better, the indistinction between animal and human'. 'The simplicity of the Tuscan language in *Pinocchio*,' the author continues, 'arises from the fact that Collodi was transmitting an esoteric truth

---

2 That Collodi was not really a mason has been demonstrated by Daniela Marcheschi, among other places in the Introduction to Collodi (1995).

and could only express it thus, as he would narrate it to a child. It is the restraint with which one speaks of unspeakable things that produces this peculiar language, in Collodi as in Apuleius.' Even the name Pinocchio, like every proper name in the book, has an esoteric meaning:

> In Latin *pinocolus* means 'bit of pine'. For a pagan it is the evergreen tree that defies winter's death. Lucignolo is a poor man's Lucifer, suitable for a *puer*, which is to say pre-initiate, and the Cat and the Fox are Legba and Eshu, great personages of African mythology who are also found in Vodou. At the time, people read such things, and the America of the late 1800s was full of books on Vodou. Some Mason from across the ocean could have informed Collodi. The life of the lodge is very strange, it is secret and full of encounters. (Zolla 2002)

All the episodes, characters and animals invented by Collodi are actually ancient symbols:

> The archetype of death and rebirth seemingly returns, always and everywhere, clothing itself in the symbolic form of being swallowed in the stomach of a whale or in the sufferings of an ass or in the green serpent that

is frightening but possesses the secret of rebirth. [. . .] The green serpent is the true guardian of trans-mutation and rebirth. It is an immemorial symbol. It appears in Claudian as a symbol of eternity in the cave of Nature, as well as of all the terrors that await the one who wants to free himself from limits and fetters, to be reborn, precisely. Collodi has his puppet declare that *Pinocchio* itself has these features when he must dress up as guard dog: 'Oh if only I could be born all over again!' (chap. 21). Therefore Pinocchio cannot escape the classic tests of water with the shipwreck, of fire at the fisherman's house, of air during the flight of the Pigeon or Spirit. I don't believe there is an episode of *Pinocchio* that cannot be traced back to that curious world that is alchemical iconography. The Land of Barn Owls? It is what one crosses to go into the Eternal Wisdom, as the first vignette of Khunrath's *Ampitheatrum aeternae sapientiae* informs us. The field of which the cat and the fox tell stories? Which Collodi calls precisely the 'blessed field' or 'field of miracles'? Find it in the *Mutus liber*, the masterpiece of French alchemical literature. (Zolla 1992: 435–36)

The motif of taking up ancient initiatory archetypes returns
unfailingly in the interpretation of the story of the puppet:

> The puppet and the ass are equivalent versions of the
> same archetype: the difficulty of victory over purely
> natural and mechanical conditions. The one is used by
> Marcus Aurelius, the other by Apuleius, to the same
> end. Collodi made use of both. Laborious victory!
> Collodi shows how, in order to obtain it, one must
> renounce all faith in human institutions and liberate
> oneself entirely from the illusion of justice and utopia.
> (Zolla 1992: 440–41)

The error of esotericism is not in the concepts that it
suggests to the interpreter—that of initiation above all (but
not alone) is decidedly pertinent. That 'the archetype of
life and rebirth' returns here as well, clothed 'in the symbolic
form of being swallowed in the stomach of a whale' or in
Pinocchio's metamorphosis into an ass, is certainly true.
The error consists rather in considering initiation to be a secret
doctrine, which is revealed to some—the initiated—and
hidden from the profane. Esotericism is acceptable, only if we
understand that the esoteric is the quotidian and the quotidian
the esoteric. Collodi invents poetically, he does not apply a

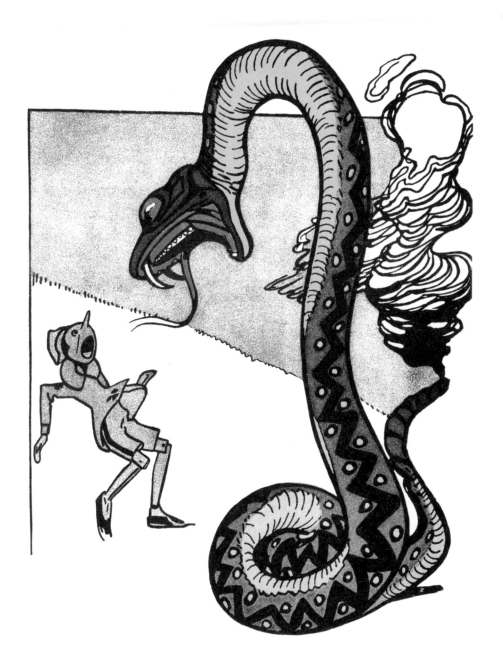

Masonic doctrine that was transmitted to him by imprudent initiates. Both in the Eleusinian mysteries and in those of the puppet it is not a matter of communicating an arcane secret that it is later forbidden to divulge to outsiders. It is in living his puppet adventures—the sale of the alphabet book, the entrance into the Grand Theatre, the flight into the Land of Toys, the encounter with the Cat and the Fox, the transformation into a donkey and the voyage into the stomach of the Dogfish—that Pinocchio, like Lucius in Apuleius, is initiated, but that to which he is initiated is his life itself. In the latter, that which initiates and that to which one is initiated mingle together and cannot in any way be distinguished, as the esoteric reading would like. The sole content of the initiation is that now there is nothing more to understand, that we have finished with having to understand, with continuing to draw water with a leaky jar. But this is precisely what the initiates at Eleusis, after having contemplated disparate objects—a child's top, a mirror, a male member, an ear of grain—and murmured senseless nursery rhymes, could not say. Just as Pinocchio cannot say it at the end of his initiation: 'Amidst all these marvels which followed one upon the other, Pinocchio himself did not know whether he was truly awake or still dreaming with his eyes open' (chap. 36).

In our reading of the fairy tale narrated by Collodi, we will therefore not expunge, as Manganelli seems to want to do with his misprint, the theme of initiation, but we will eliminate from it all traces of esotericism. There is, as Benjamin knew, a 'profane illumination' that introduces us, beyond all esotericism, into that 'image space' in which body and imagination interpenetrate (Benjamin 1977: 217), and with respect to which it does not make sense to emphasize 'the mysterious side of the mysterious' (216). It is in this space that Pinocchio's fairy tale moves, on condition that we know how to recognize 'the everyday as impenetrable and the impenetrable as everyday' (216). If symbols and archetypes incessantly return, if they do nothing but put on new figures each time, this is not by way of a doctrine: it is the imagination that lives in them and through them, and it can evoke them at will just as much in a sacred book—the Bible—as in a humble fairy tale for children. Like profane illumination, the imagination does not know hierarchy and is frankly ignorant of every distinction between the sacred and the profane, to which it does nothing but stir it up and confound it. And we will do so as well, with the authorization of superior principles.

Once upon a time there was . . .

'A king!' my little readers will say straight away.

No, children, you are mistaken. Once upon a time there was a piece of wood. (chap. 1)

The parallel commentator rightly sees a provocation in this 'catastrophic beginning' (Manganelli 2002: 11). If 'once upon a time' is 'the highway, the signpost, the password for the world of fairy tale', in this case 'the road is illusory, the sign is lacking, the word is twisted' (11). The teller of tales, in this case Collodi, with his opening swindle, has given access to the place of fairy tale, but of a fairy tale that is no longer such, 'dramatically incompatible with the other royal and ancient land of fairy tale, certified by the golden circle of a crown' (11). We could

actually be dealing with an 'attempt to kill the fairy tale' (12).

In a short story written many years before in a newspaper that he ran, *Il lampione* [The lamp post],[3] Collodi had already mocked the fairy tale's incipit, if not to 'kill the fairy tale', then at least to oppose it to history:

> In recounting to you a short story, my beloved readers, I will not begin as servants begin—One upon a time there was a king—because once upon a time there were no kings, and whether it was better or worse than now I don't know, and if you want to know then go seek it out in history. (Marcheschi 1990)

In any case, the king is something that seems to be constitutively lacking.

The parallel glossator, who has a special relationship with the figure of the capitalized King—as the tormenting pages of the chapter of the same title in his *Agli dèi ulteriori* [To those gods beyond] testify, it is a matter of a true and proper identification (Manganelli 2014a)—concentrates his analyses at this point on the peculiar modality of the nonexistence of the King. The King has chosen not to exist, because he has discovered that ' "nonexistence" is his typical and unassailable form of existing' (Manganelli 2002: 12). If we attempt, instead,

---

3 Collodi's short story was published in *Il Lampione*, 18 October 1848; but one can more easily read it in Marcheschi (1990).

to follow our initial intuition on the special literary status of the fairy tale of the puppet, we can draw from it some not very reassuring conclusions. The story of Pinocchio is a fairy tale, which opens by denying that it is one. 'Once upon a time there was a piece of wood' is not the beginning of a fairy tale—all the more since, as it is immediately specified, we are not dealing with a luxurious piece of wood, but 'just a bit of firewood, like the ones that people use to light a fire in the stove or on the hearth to warm their rooms in winter' (chap. 1). The evocation of an indoor setting among commonplace things decisively dislocates the narrative from the land of the fairy tale to that of a realistic sketch, to which the two comforting and not at all fabular figures of Mastr'Antonio, called Maestro Cherry, and Geppetto, called Polendina, are perfectly suited. And yet the just-negated fairy tale violently breaks forth as soon as the piece of fire wood reveals itself as the most fantastic of all the fairy-tale creatures that have ever existed.

Roland Jakobson and Pëtr Bogatyrëv, in an exemplary study on 'Folklore as a Special Form of Creativity', translated the fundamental opposition between myth and oral culture on the one hand and the literary work and scripture on the other, in terms of the linguistic opposition between *langue* and *parole.* The work of folklore—to which the fairy tale belongs by right—is a fact of *langue*, which reciters, insofar as they can always transform it, receive and transmit in an impersonal way. For the author of a literary work, this latter represents instead a fact of *parole*, which must be invented from scratch each time and presupposes an author and not only a reciter.

Whether or not he was aware of this, Collodi, with unexpected skill, played his card between myth and literature, between the fairy tale and the short story (or the novel). He places in the hands of the reader a fable that is not a fable and a novel that is not a novel, but shows itself to be more fantastic than any fairy tale. And it is likely that the success of the book, which in a few years reached 700,000 copies, was owed precisely to the boldness with which it calls into question the taken-for-granted opposition between myth and the literary work and reminds us that they are not two separate substances, but only two tensions in the single magnetic field of imagination and language. That the protagonist should moreover be neither an animal nor a human being, but a puppet, corresponds perfectly to the hybrid status of the narrative of his adventures.

What is a fable? In Greek, the word for fable is *ainos* or, more commonly, *mythos*. And it is by this latter term, 'myth', that Socrates designates it in the *Phaedo*, shortly before his death, evoking, alongside music and philosophy, precisely this peculiar poetic genre and the name of its inventor par excellence: Aesop. To Cebes and the friends who are standing around him, Socrates recounts a dream that he happened to have dreamt many times, now in this form, now in another, in which a voice stubbornly enjoined him: 'Socrates, make music!' (60e). At first it had seemed to him that the dream was inciting him to do what he was already doing, as one does with runners, since philosophy is in fact the supreme music; but then, on reflection, he was convinced that the dream was asking him to compose music of a more popular kind and that he must not disobey it in this.

> So I first wrote in honour of the god of the present festival. After that I realized that a poet, if he is to be a poet, must compose fables (*mythous*), not arguments (*logous*). Being no teller of fables (*mythologikos*) myself, I took the stories I knew and had at hand, the fables of Aesop, and I versified the first ones I came across. (61c)

Which fables these were, we are not told. A little before, while massaging his legs, which were sore from his bonds, Socrates, though without defining it, nonetheless tells us something about the nature of the fable, observing that the pain he previously experienced was changing into its opposite, into pleasure.

> What a strange thing that which men call pleasure seems to be, and how astonishing the relation it has with what is thought to be its opposite, namely pain! A man cannot have both at the same time. Yet if he pursues and catches the one, he is almost always bound to catch the other too, like two creatures with one head. I think that if Aesop had noted this he would have composed a fable that a god wished to reconcile their opposition but could not do so, so he joined together (*synepsen*) their two heads, and therefore when a man has the one, the other follows later. (60c)

It is possible that Aristotle had this passage from the *Phaedo* in mind when he defines a riddle (*ainigma*, a term related to one of the words for fable, *ainos*) as a 'joining together (*synapsai*, the same verb used by Socrates) of impossible things when speaking of real things' (*Poetics* 1458a 24–26), and when, in the

Rhetoric, he classifies the fable among examples and parables, namely among discourses founded on analogy, which hit on similarities where there do not seem to be any (1393a 25–30). In any case, what Plato has Socrates say is that the structure of the fable is founded on the reversal of a thing into its contrary and on an ambiguity so consubstantial that it is never possible to grasp a thing without its contrary. In the two fables that Plato invents, that of the cicadas in the *Phaedrus* and that on the origin of Eros in the *Symposium*, ambiguity and reversal are equally present: the joy of song among the cicadas is reversed into death by starvation, and the genealogy of Eros is nothing but a series of contraries linked together, who knows how: poor/rich, ignorant/wise, mortal/immortal. In the same way, in Aesop's fables, the positive winds up producing the negative and every action produces an effect contrary to the one intended: the donkey who dresses in lion skins to frighten the fox betrays himself by braying; Thales falls into a well because he insisted on contemplating the stars; the donkey who wanted to live on dew, in imitation of the cicadas, dies of hunger.

It is not surprising that the fable of Pinocchio, precisely like the one imagined by Socrates, plays out from beginning to end by means of a series of unexpected reversals and incessant crossings from one contrary to another. There is not a good intention that does not result in mischief, nor a mishap or misfortune that does not turn out to be an escape or salvation. And so in the end, if one must have recourse to the formula that concludes Aesop's fables (*ho mythos deloi*, the fable shows . . .), the only moral is that nothing is what it is: the wood is not wood, nor the friend friend, nor the donkey donkey, nor fairy fairy, nor cricket cricket, but everything changes and continually transforms.

Cristina Campo, a writer whom the parallel glossator characterizes as 'regal', does not name Pinocchio in her extraordinary digressions on the fairy tale. And yet, when she situates the fairy tale in 'a middle province [. . .] between trial and liberation', in which good and evil 'exchange masks' (Campo 1987), and when she defines the fairy tale's hero through his simultaneous belonging to two worlds, in one of which the hero must somehow know how to read the other in filigree, it is difficult not to think of the marvellous puppet. Precisely the peculiar position of the character (to define him as a 'hero' would be too much) between these two worlds furnishes the key to understanding the fairy tale and, at the same time, permits us to verify its relation to initiation. What

happens in an initiation is that a human and earthly element—
the life of a human being—becomes the vehicle of a superhuman or divine event, in which it somehow participates.
However, it is not in any way a question—we must repeat it
yet again against the esoteric interpretation—of a teaching or
a doctrine, but of something like an impression or a 'passion'
in the etymological sense. 'The initiates,' writes Aristotle in
one of the fragments of his lost dialogue *On Philosophy*, 'do
not have to learn something (*mathein ti*), but after having
become capable, they undergo it (*pathein*) and are disposed to
it' (*De philosophia* frag. 15; Aristotle 1952: 87). The same holds
for the protagonist of the fairy tale, who, in his marvellous
vicissitudes, does not attain a doctrine or a higher knowledge,
but goes through emotions and astonishments whose meaning
escapes him point by point. In fact, if it is possible to further
characterize the fairy tale with respect to initiation, he does
not precisely read 'that world above in filigree', as Cristina
Campo suggests, by complying with 'its secret laws in his
choices, in his refusals' (Campo 1987); instead he frees himself
in some way from the initiatory rite, by undergoing it like a
spell. They are a hex and a bewitchment to take speech away
from him, and this bewitchment is, to the same extent, a being
set free from the mystery, a sleepwalking but unreserved

I.

Come andò che Maestro Ciliegia, falegname, trovó un pezzo di legno, che piangeva e rideva come un bambino.

surrendering of himself to the little tricks of magic. Pinocchio is not an initiate, not even when he is transformed into a boy: of the experiences he has lived as a puppet, he does not know what to say at the end other than: 'How funny I was when I was a puppet!' (chap. 36). Funny, only funny—as in a farce or a joke in which there is precisely nothing to understand.

Károly Kerényi and, after him, Reinhold Merkelbach have shown that between the pagan mysteries and the ancient novel there was a genetic link, that, in the last analysis, the novel derives in this sense from mystery. Exactly as in the mysteries, in the novel an individual life is placed in correspondence with a divine or, in any case, superhuman element, in such a way that the vicissitudes and tergiversations of an ordinary existence take on a special significance and become mysterious in their turn. Just as the initiates in the dim Eleusinian light bore witness to the mimed evocation of the abduction of Kore into Hades and her reappearance on earth in spring and, in this way, believed they had caught a glimpse of a hope of salvation for their life as well, those who, deeply moved, follow the plot that the novel weaves around its characters participate in some way in their destiny and insert their existence into a mystery. It goes without saying that the novel's initiation is not a sacred mystery, that it can even concern a life that, like Emma Bovary's, has entirely lost its mystery. Nevertheless, in this case as well, there will be an initiation all the same, even if a miserable one, even if to nothing other than life itself and its dissipation.

From this perspective, how should we look at the novel about Pinocchio? Calvino, with his usual acumen, has suggested that we are actually dealing with a picaresque novel, 'a book of wandering and hunger, of poorly patronized inns, cops and gallows' (Calvino 2007). If this is true, the puppet would be a *pícaro matriculado* [downright rascal], an extreme reincarnation of Lazarillo and Guzmán de Alfarache, of Simplicissimus and Gil Blas. That his adventures are, like those

of the *pícaros*, a hopeless series of disasters and a not very edifying rascalhood is granted; but Pinocchio is a *pícaro* in a more intimate and profound sense. Americo Castro has seen the origin of the *pícaro* in the insecure and contradictory condition of the converted Jews who remained in Spain after the expulsion (both Mateo Alemán, the author of *Guzmán*, and the author of *Celestina*, Fernando de Rojas, were converted Jews) and put it in relation with what is for him the fundamental characteristic of Spanish existence: *vivir disviviéndose*, living while disavowing any sense of a life of one's own. Like the *pícaro*, Pinocchio can live only by de-living [*disvivendo*], by stubbornly lacking and fleeing his own life. How, then, can there be an initiation not to a life, but to a de-living? The answer to this question—if it were possible to find—would define once and for all the essence and meaning of the puppet's adventures. And, perhaps, of every human adventure on earth.

Collodi, like his parallel glossator—who confesses that he feels for this literary genre 'a sentiment closer to repugnance than to simple annoyance' (Manganelli 1994)—could not stand novels, especially those of his contemporaries with social pretensions, and hoped for the reappearance in his time of a 'Dr Cervantes', who would know how to cure us of what he considered a true and proper disease, unfortunately still in the acute phase, and 'wise doctors like Cervantes come out with the remedy only when the disease is coming to an end' (Collodi 1948: 789). It is possible that Pinocchio was precisely that remedy, intended to imbue with new life a nearly irremediably senescent form. In any case, whether or not it is a novel, *Pinocchio* is not, as Pancrazi maintained, a masterpiece written by chance. Collodi shows in fact that he is able to reflect conscientiously on the form of writing that he practices, and in the singular hodgepodge of a railway guide and narrative that is *Un romanzo in vapore* [A novel in steam] he puts in the mouth of an unidentified Professor Pagliano—who, if he had not been the inventor of a 'purifying Syrup', would have been 'the inventor of the social novel in Italy'—a parodic, witty theory of the novel. There is in fact, according to the professor, a certain analogy between the Syrup and the contemporary novel, because 'in this world everything is Syrup' and every art—even literature—'has its secrets and its recipes'. The novelist's 'big secret' lies first of all in preventing the reader from yawning, 'nodding off', and the sleep of boredom, 'which, in many cases, believe me, is much deeper than that of innocence'. It is a matter of 'knowing how to excite curiosity and being able to enchain the reader in some way or another to the pages of the book, to be able to draw them along, like so many slaves, yoked to the chariot of fantasy' (Collodi 2010: 143).

The example that follows of a novel composed according to Professor Pagliano's recipe holds some surprises. First, the opening of the first chapter is reminiscent of the false beginning of the sixth chapter of *Pinocchio* in Manganelli's version: 'It was a cold, dark, rainy winter's night' ('When it comes to novels,' the professor comments, 'it is always good to stick to bad weather!'; Collodi 2010: 144). The recipe of the novelistic Syrup is quickly stated: one must conclude every chapter with an interjection of surprise (Ah!) and, instead of supplying in the next one a reasonable explanation for the reader's curiosity, introduce a new unexpected event, which will conclude in its turn with a new interjection (Eh!) that will keep the curiosity of the reader unsatisfied, and so on until the end, always jumping 'from one topic to another [. . .] drawing along the poor reader who, shrugging his shoulders, will be content to exclaim at the end of each chapter—Uhm!' (145).

It is easy to recognize—in this recipe that, 'with five interjections paced out', assembles a 'social novel to be read avidly from the frontispiece to the last page of the index' (Collodi 2010: 145)—a parody of the principle of composition of the

Adventures of a Puppet: to Professor Pagliano's interjections and reversals there correspond Pinocchio's 'buts', which always announce an unforeseen event and, proceeding from one topic to another, draw along readers 'yoked to the chariot of fantasy' (143).

According to the esoteric interpretation, Collodi's novel begins with a 'prologue in heaven', in which 'the contrast between the cosmic Demiurge and the heavenly Father, also narrated in gnostic cosmogonies' is displayed (Zolla 1994: 431). In reality, the prologue does not seem as if it happens in heaven, but is situated, more modestly, first 'in the workshop of an old carpenter' (who is none other than Mastr'Antonio, called Maestro Cherry because of his shiny purple nose; chap. 1) and then in a 'basement room lit by a skylight under the front steps' (Geppetto's house; chap. 3).

The fact is that the creation of Pinocchio happens in two steps—it is, like that of Adam, a double creation. Theologians have asked for almost two millennia why the creation of our progenitors took place twice: once in Genesis 1:27 and again in Genesis 2:7. To give an appearance of technicity, biblical philologists call the first creation 'Elohist' and the second 'Yahwist'; but what is essential is that, in the first, God creates man in his image and likeness, 'male and female he created them' (1:27), and entrusted to them dominion 'over the fish of the sea and over the birds of the air and over every living thing that moves upon the earth' (1:28), but the text says nothing about how Elohim went about his work; in the second, by contrast, the creation of Adam is described concisely but fully: God moulds the man from the clay of the earth and breathes into his nostrils to infuse him with life, before placing him in the garden of Eden.

Origen furnishes an explanation of this double creation that has the merit of simplicity. The first creation, in the image of God, refers to the soul, and the second, which derives from guilt, to the body moulded from clay and earth. Two centuries later, a Palestinian theologian, author of a commentary on Genesis called a 'catena' or chain, because every verse is, so to speak, chained on the page to its glosses, adds to the first two also a third creation, which happens when God clothes Adam and Eve in garments of animal skins before driving them out of the earthly paradise: 'The allegorists,' writes Procopius of Gaza, whose name seems to allude to the 'progress' (*prokopē*) of his interminable chains, 'affirm that the man made in the image is to signify the soul; but the one moulded from the clay signifies the body that is subtle and worthy to dwell in paradise, which some have called luminous; finally the garments of skins refer to the body in flesh and bone' (Migne 1865: 221A, 222A). A trace of this third creation in the story of Pinocchio is when Geppetto, before making the puppet leave the house to send him to school, dresses him from head to toe ('he made him a little suit of flowered paper, a pair of shoes of tree bark and a cap fashioned out of bread crumb', chap. 8).

At least at first glance, the biblical text—Elohist or Yahwist as the case may be—has nothing to do with the double creation of Pinocchio. In the workshop of Maestro Cherry no creation properly happens, and this has caused the parallel commentator to suppose that the piece of wood turned up there by mistake. There is, according to Manganelli, a conflict between destination and destiny: the old carpenter is the ' "mistaken addressee [*destinario*]", whose task is to render the piece of wood conscious of its destiny' (Manganelli 2002: 15). In this sense, the sojourn of the piece of wood in Maestro Cherry's workshop would be only a prelude—and a transitory and faulty one—to the true creation, which takes place only in Geppetto's house.

A more attentive reading shows that the first chapter is instead rich with implications of every kind, philosophical and theological no less than literary. Above all that it 'turned up [*capitò*]': 'one fine day this piece of wood'—it was previously explained that it is not a question of 'expensive wood', but a simple 'bit of firewood'—'turned up in the workshop of an old carpenter' (chap. 1). 'Whatever does it mean that it turns up?' asks the parallel commentator, and he suggests that 'the piece of wood had chosen to go to that workshop', perhaps because it had resolved itself 'to a transformation, a birth' (Manganelli 2002: 14). Of this 'turned up' another reading is naturally also possible, which could interest a theorist of the fallen [*discenditiva*] nature of man like Manganelli,[4] and it is that the firewood was 'cast down' into the world, independently of its will, according to a model of creation and birth that is already present in the Church Fathers. 'Scripture', notes Origen again, 'indicates the creation with the new and peculiar term *katabolē*. [. . .] But *katabolē* in Greek means rather "to cast down" (*deicere*), "to cast from above" (*deorsum iacere*), and Latin translators have improperly translated it "creation" ' (Book III,

---

4 The term *discenditiva* is a coinage of Manganelli's, which does not necessarily imply the traditional Christian view of the Fall. (I owe this reference to Carlo Salzani.) [Trans.]

chap. 5, §4). It is likely that this originary meaning of the word was recalled by a twentieth-century philosopher, when he defines the human condition with the term 'being thrown', flung down.

Someone (God?) threw the piece of wood down into the carpenter's workshop, which is to say into the world, so that the demiurge could make from it a living being, and the heedless Maestro Cherry instead thinks only of using it to make a leg for a little table out of it. At this point, everything is inverted and the first creation of Pinocchio is revealed to be a creation in reverse. 'Wood' is, in Greek, the name of the matter, *hylē*, to which the demiurge was to give form. Commenting on the *Timaeus*, which according to the ancients contained Plato's theory of matter, an obscure glossator, perhaps a Jew, of whom we know just his name, Calcidius, therefore translates the Greek *hylē* (and the other terms that, according to him, Plato used to express matter) with the word *silva*, wood, forest. As a branch plucked from some tree, the future Pinocchio—as Manganelli recalls many times—has an arboreal and sylvan nature; he is, in this sense, 'matter'. Nonetheless, not only is the old carpenter not in a position to give form to his wooden matter, which he does not even manage to touch at

first, but it is the wood, the *hylē*, that models and forms him to its pleasure, transforming him first into a 'gargoyle', with his tongue 'hanging down to his chin', and finally striking him as if by lighting, to the point of transfiguration ('poor Maestro Cherry fell over as if he had been struck by lightning. [. . .] His face looked transformed, and even the end of his nose, instead of its usual purple colour, had turned blue from fright'; chap. 1). And the piece of wood—like the god of the Bible—achieves this creation in reverse, in which it is matter that gives form to the demiurge, with its voice alone, which is, in fact, a 'little, tiny voice' similar to that of a child, which speaks three times: first when the carpenter has raised his arm into the air with the axe, pleading him, 'Don't hit me too hard!', then complaining when the axe hits him ('Ouch! You hurt me!') and, finally, when the carpenter begins to plane it up and down, laughing while mumbling, 'Stop it! You're tickling me all over!' (chap. 1).

It is appropriate to linger on the singular relationship between the inept demiurge and the 'little voice' of his matter. For some reason, Maestro Cherry stubbornly insists on not considering it properly a voice that utters words ('it's clear that I must have imagined that little voice,' he twice repeats), but a lament and a cry ('Could it be this piece of wood, by any chance, that has learned to cry and lament like a child?'). Even though the wood has not cried or lamented, but only 'pleaded' and 'complained' in words, the carpenter a little later beats it 'mercilessly [*senza carità*]'—that is, without love—'to find out whether there was any little voice lamenting'. And it is perhaps precisely because he seeks in its voice only a cry and a lament that he cannot fail to be thunderstruck when the wood speaks to him for the third time while laughing ('he heard the same little voice laughing and saying [. . .]'; chap. 1). Like creation, which 'is groaning in labour pains' in Romans 8:22, *hylē*, sylvan, woody matter, cannot speak—much less laugh—but can only lament.

Ernesto de Martino has devoted a well-known study to the lament as a ritual cry for the dead. Like every rite, lamentation has the goal of confronting the crisis of presence caused by the death of a relative. It unfolds in two moments: the inarticulate cry, in which mourning seems to yield 'to convulsive discharges, stunned stupor, destructive fury' (Martino 2021: 220), which the ecclesiastical sources describe as a 'diabolical song' (215), and the true and proper ritual lamentation, in which the threat of a collapse of presence is warded off and the cry is returned 'to the horizon of discourse'

(247). The confused voice and formless screams thus pass over into the articulated word. If Maestro Cherry cannot form his piece of wood, it is therefore because, caught up in the lament as 'diabolical song', he rejects the idea that matter could speak to him and be somehow already alive. This denial of the future puppet's word not only inhibits his demiurgic faculty but puts him at the mercy of the matter that he was to have formed. Creation is inverted, because the old demiurge stubbornly insists on misunderstanding as lament what, by all evidence, is an unequivocal power of speech.

If laments are always in some way funeral laments, what or whose death is Pinocchio crying about? In the book, the first death is certainly the Talking Cricket, who, struck with a mallet, remains 'stuck to the wall stone dead' (chap. 4—even if it must be an apparent death, because later we again encounter him alive and healthy). The verb 'to die' appears a few pages later, but refers to the hunger that torments the puppet ('If my pa was here, I wouldn't be dying of yawning now!'; chap. 5). The place, very near Geppetto's house, where the starving Pinocchio arrives 'in a hundred hops' is a land of the dead ('The shops were shut; the doors of the houses were shut; and, in the street, there wasn't even a dog to be seen. It looked like the land of the dead'; chap. 6—hell, then?); and the verb 'to die' reappears further on, when Mangiafuoco threatens to use the puppet to 'give a lovely, bright flame for the roast', and the latter invokes Geppetto: 'Papa, Papa, save me! I don't want to die. No, no, I don't want to die!' (chap. 10); and shortly afterward when he offers himself instead to be thrown into the flames because poor Harlequin 'should' not 'die' for him (chap. 11). Hanged by the murderers, Pinocchio feels 'half-dead' and then actually dies—but not effectually ('He closed his eyes, opened his mouth, straightened his legs and, giving a great shudder, hung there as if frozen stiff'; chap. 15).

In the novel, the *locus classicus* of death is, however, certainly the 'cottage as white as snow', in which there lives only a 'beautiful little girl, with blue hair and a face as white as a wax image', who declares that in that house 'everyone is dead' and adds, with an indisputable contradiction, that she is dead too (chap. 15). Nonetheless it is in this same cemeterial house that the little girl rises again as a fairy, to attend to the resurrection of Pinocchio, which is moreover announced by a crow and a little owl in medical garb ('When a corpse weeps, it's a sign that he is beginning to recover', 'when a corpse weeps, it's a sign that he is sorry to die'; chap. 16). And in his penultimate adventure, Pinocchio dies by drowning as a donkey, only to unexpectedly return to the surface as a wooden puppet.

The status of death in Collodi's fairy tale is equivocal and controversial: all or nearly all the characters are at once living and dead, like the shades of the pagan Hades, which drink blood and speak, and the damned in the Christian hell, who suffer and experience anger and spite like the living. Perhaps the novel's season is truly in hell, and it is possible that Manganelli recalled this in his infernal treatise of 1985, where the protagonist 'assumes' that he is dead, but cannot be sure, and when he communicates his hypothesis to an anonymous inhabitant of the place ('I suppose I am dead. What do you say?'), we hear the reply: 'A good supposition, certainly; but I couldn't tell you more.' The anonymous interlocutor wondered about his death, but 'did not come to any conclusion'; the fact is that for those who find themselves in that place (that it is hell is also only a probable supposition, it could also just be literature), it is 'manifestly absurd to call themselves living' (Manganelli 2014b), even if no one can prove they are dead.

Phaedrus, an author for whom the parallel commentator has a particular fondness, has drawn up a genealogy of the fable that it is worth the trouble of reflecting on. According to this author who is fully aware of his ingenuity, of whose life we know absolutely nothing, the fable, or better the *fabella*, is a cunning attempt by slaves to say what they cannot say without incurring punishments and whippings: 'slaves subjected to guilt (*obnoxia*), because they did not dare to say what they would have liked, transposed their sufferings into *fabellae* and evaded the accusation (*calumnia*) by pretending to joke (*fictis iocis*)' (*Fabulae Aesopiae*, Book 3, 'Phaedrus ad Eutychum', ll. 34–37). *Obnoxia* is a technical term in Roman law and means 'subjected to *noxa*', to the gravest guilt, which can lead to death (*nex*). The fable is thus a stratagem to escape guilt and death. With its made-up jokes, it escapes *calumnia*, the false, lethal accusation that hangs over everyone, in particular the weak and insecure, who are thus inclined to allow themselves to be accused and even to accuse themselves, as Pinocchio does. It is possible that, to liberate themselves from guilt, they must make themselves dead or, in any case, de-live their own life in a zone in which the difference between the living and the dead dissolves to the point of confusion. By becoming *fabella*, their life escapes guilt, but consigns itself, as innocent, to a singular Acheron, inhabited by puppets, fairies and other creatures neither dead nor living.

(Collodi has read his Phaedrus: the episode in which Pinocchio, as guard dog, rejects the bargain proposed by the martens, repeats point-by-point the fable of the 'Canis fidelis'

39

[Faithful dog]; and the buyer who wants to skin the puppet transformed into a donkey so that he can make a drum with his skin recalls the Celts who, in the fable 'Asinus et Galli' [The donkey and the priests of Cybele], with the skin of their old donkey *sibi fecerunt tympana* [made a drum for themselves]: 'after death he believed he would be at peace / now that he is dead he always takes a beating' [*Fabulae Aesopiae*, Book 4, 'Asinus et Galli', ll. 7–11].)

That the creation in the carpenter's workshop could not be a creation follows from other incontrovertible reasons as well. The piece of wood not only speaks, but gives proof of having at its disposal at least two senses: despite not yet having eyes, it sees clearly, since it immediately perceives the gesture of the carpenter when he lifts the axe, and as to touch, he is sensitive both to pain and to the 'tickling' from planing. Matter is alive, or as medieval philosophers often said, it inchoately contains in itself all forms, and only a demiurge who is aware of this can collaborate with their liberation. In any case Mastr'Antonio—we can now restore his name to him, seeing that his nose is no longer purple—is not capable of it, and with the voice and laughter of matter, which are the true protagonists of the episode, he has absolutely nothing to do. There

remains only his blue nose: an omen of the puppet's dispro-
portionate nose and, due to its fresh colouring, an incongruous
and neglected clue to the fairy-girl's hair.

In any case, in the second creation in Geppetto's house,
the faculty of speech, which the piece of wood exercised
wholeheartedly in the carpenter's
workshop, seems to abruptly
fail him. Pinocchio,
as Geppetto has
willed to

call him, remains for the entire third chapter stubbornly mute. Even when the demiurge, who has 'quickly shaped his hair, then his forehead, then his eyes', seeing that the eyes 'were moving and staring straight at him', directs his speech at him 'with a resentful note', he does not respond ('Nobody replied'; chap. 3). Pinocchio laughs at him, 'teases' him—presumably in the form of sneers and grimaces, as when Geppetto shouts at him: 'Stop your laughing!'—and he sticks out his tongue, but he does not utter words. As soon as he has arms and hands, he steals his Polendina wig and puts it on his own head, but always without the banter that had so frightened his first demiurge.

It is possible that the puppet has good reasons for his insolent silence. Perhaps Geppetto is not the good man he seems to be, who with his insipid meekness will later succeed in overcoming Pinocchio's cautious reticence. He is rather, if we want to call once more on the testimony of the discredited esoteric reading, the evil demiurge of the Gnostics, the ill-fated architect of creation. The first violence he exercised on 'his puppet' is to impose a name on him: 'I'd like to call him Pinocchio. It's a name that will bring him good luck. I once knew a whole Pinocchio family: father Pinocchio, mother Pinocchia, and the Pinocchi children, and they all did well for themselves. The richest was a beggar' (chap. 3). It is difficult to imagine a more aloof malice: by giving a name to a piece of wood he has not only taken away his innocence but, by naming him in that way, he cunningly condemns him to misery and bad luck.

Geppetto's bonhomie and Pinocchio's impertinence are so taken for granted that no one seems to have noted that it is he, the affable Polendina, who is the first to rudely address the puppet ('with a resentful note') who naïvely looks at him: 'Old wooden eyes, why are you looking at me?' (chap. 3). And when the puppet, for whom he has just made his mouth, starts laughing, it is 'with a threatening voice' that he orders him to stop it. But his most suspicious imposture, his most arrogant trick is the pretence to declare himself the father of the puppet whom he has been limited to 'carving and fabricating' with his tools: 'You scoundrel of a son! I haven't finished making you, and you are already showing little respect for your father!' If Pinocchio, hearing himself called son, gives him a kick 'on the end of his nose' (again a nose!), if as soon as he stretches his legs, he slips out the front door and takes to his heels, it is possible to see in these irreverent gestures and in that obstinate silence the just reaction of the creature who turns away, horrified by his perverse demiurge.

In the eyes of the esotericist, the no-holds-barred fight between Maestro Cherry and Geppetto that occupies the second chapter ('they grabbed each other, scratching, biting and mauling each other') can therefore appear as a fight between the good god external to creation and the wicked demiurge, creator and lord of the world. And, according to all evidence and notwithstanding the traditional reading, the role of the obscure agent of evil would fall precisely to the one who usurped the name father. And the principle that, in the puppet, obstinately rebels against Geppetto's directives is that parcel or sliver of light that, according to the fanciful Gnostic mythopoesis unconsciously and felicitously operating in Collodi's mind, has remained imprisoned in its wooden matter.

Adventures

In the *Giornale per i bambini* (Newspaper for children; edited by Ferdinando Martini, and printed, ominously, in Rome every Thursday, at 130 Piazza Montecitorio, starting in 1881, exactly ten years after the inauguration of parliament) the title read simply: 'The Story of a Puppet'. A cartoon immediately below the title inexplicably shows a cat that has clambered onto a clock that reads exactly a quarter after five, but the five is where we would expect to find a seven. On the frontispiece of the first edition (1883), illustrated by Enrico Mazzanti for Felice Paggi, a bookseller-publisher on Via del Proconsolo in Florence, one reads instead: *The Adventures of Pinocchio*, while the original title has become a subtitle, in smaller print: *The Story of a Puppet*. No longer a story, thus, nor a tale, nor a fable: 'adventures' rather, with a term that from its first appearance in Romance languages signifies both an event and the tale that hands it down: *Ici commence l'aventure* [here begins the adventure], according to an incipit that has today become all too taken for granted. But 'adventure' originally means the same thing as 'destiny', 'fate': 'An adventure that has to take place / cannot be prevented / and something that has to happen / cannot fail to do so for any reason,' one reads in a romance in Old French (*Roman de Rou*, ll. 5609–12, quoted in Agamben 2018: 29). At once event, tale and destiny, it is not surprising that adventure becomes for the *Minnesänger* a beautiful maiden, *frau Aventiure*, who seeks to enter into the poet's heart to tell him 'wonderful things' (*von wunder sagen*—and who knows whether the fairy with blue hair may not be a final figure of 'lady adventure', at once a living creature and a tale).

In any case, after the celestial-infernal prologue, the true and proper adventure of Pinocchio begins when the puppet, after he stretches the legs carved by Geppetto, flees, running out of the house. Decisive here is the first character to whom adventure-destiny hands him over: a carabiniere,[1] who 'courageously planted himself, feet apart, in the middle of the road,

---

1 The representative of one of two Italian law-enforcement agencies, which, unlike the civilian *polizia*, is officially part of the military and therefore represented, for many in Collodi's time, the full abusive power of the state. (I owe this clarification to Carlo Salzani.) Perella's translation retains the Italian term, while Lucas and Brock opt for the more generic 'policeman'. [Trans.]

determined to halt it and prevent the chance of any greater disaster' (chap. 3). It is the first appearance of a 'guardian of order', as the glossator calls him, whose 'socialized squalor' will return many times to lay snares for the puppet (Manganelli 2002: 31). We do well not to allow two peculiarities of this fateful encounter to escape us: the first is that the carabiniere, as is fitting for a representative of the Law, proposes to 'prevent the chance': that is to say, he is, among the contingencies of adventure, a principle contrary to them. The second detail, and even more significant, is that the carabiniere 'nearly caught him by the nose', a 'nose that looked as if it was specially made for policemen to catch hold of' (chap. 3). The nose is one of the fundamental themes of the book and, as such, it had already appeared at the moment of the puppet's second creation, when Geppetto has no sooner made the nose than it begins to grow 'and it grew and grew and grew, and in a few minutes it became a nose that never seemed to end' (chap. 3).

We must return to the motif of the nose that never ends and its relationship with truth and falsehood, but here, at the beginning of the adventure, it interests us because it seems specially made to be caught hold of by the guardians of order. *Prendere per il naso*, 'to take by the nose', in Italian commonly means 'to make a fool of, to pull someone's leg', but the original formulation is rather *menare per il naso*, 'to lead by the nose', which derives from the ring that is put in the nose of oxen to be able to lead them where one wills. In question here

X.

I burattini
riconoscono il loro
fratello Pinocchio, e gli
fanno una grandissima
festa; ma sul più bello, esce fuori
il burattinaio Mangiafoco, e Pinocchio
corre il pericolo di fare una brutta fine

is 'conduct', a technical term in the juridico-political lexicon of the West, with which the Law proposes precisely, as it is doing even now, to guide the behaviours of human beings, to secure, as one says in school, good conduct. We are therefore dealing with a principle decisively hostile to the anarchic puppet, to whom nothing is more repugnant than to feel guided or conducted, even on the right path. More generally, in the book, the Law—as is immediately obvious in the unmotivated arrest of Geppetto and, even more, in the absurd judicial code of Catchfools, which condemns to prison the one who has suffered a crime—is always a principle of abuse and oppression.

For the entire episode of Pinocchio's flight and the arrest of 'that poor man Geppetto' on the part of the carabiniere, Pinocchio has always remained religiously silent. It is not he who has his presumed papa arrested, it is the 'bystanders and loiterers' who gather in a knot around the carabiniere, the puppet and Geppetto, who wants to box him on the ears but realizes only then that 'he had forgotten to make any' (chap. 3). That the puppet can be taken by the nose, but not by the ears, says a great deal about his reticence to any linguistic persuasion; but that the demiurge had forgotten to make ears for him reminds us that he did not create with the word like the God of the Bible. He is, rather, a gnostic creator, who essentially has to do with *Sigé*, silence, 'mother', as the fanciful Valentinian sources say, 'of all those who have been emitted from the Abyss'—a very special silence, which 'has concealed what it could not speak of the unspeakable and declared incomprehensible what it has understood' (Simonetti 1970: 233). As should be obvious to the reader by now, it is not a question here of furnishing an esoteric explanation, but, in Collodi's imagination, of the stubborn, immovable incomprehension that Geppetto continually displays with respect to his 'son'.

Having hurried back home, 'just as a kid of a young hare might have done with the huntsmen after him', Pinocchio must deal with his second irksome encounter: the Talking Cricket. And, to stand up to him, he again finds speech, with 'Who's that calling me?', perfectly incongruous with respect to the '*cree-cree-cree*' of the insect, which is anything but a call. Peremptorily invited to go away, the Cricket responds that he will not leave until he has first told him 'a great truth' about children who abandon the paternal home and must later bitterly regret it. It is perhaps the word 'truth' that drives the puppet to pronounce

frankly—with a shortened nose, so to speak—
and for the first time his program of life: 'I
haven't the slightest desire to study, because
I have more fun chasing after butterflies
and climbing trees to take the baby birds
from their nests.' And it is here that the
Talking Cricket shows himself to be
a prophet, even if his prediction
is ill omened: 'if you do that, you'll
grow up to be a perfect jackass' (chap. 4). Among all the
innumerable animals that
appear in the book (chicks,
white blackbirds, falcons,
giant pigeons, dolphins,
snails, chicken-thieving
beech martens, parrots,
mastiffs who can't swim,
four mortician rabbits
'black as ink' [chap. 17],
a beautiful marmot, a
philosopher tuna, crows
and owls in medical garb,

woodpeckers, fish, and mice, as well as, of course, the Cat, the Fox, and the terrible Dogfish) the ass has a privileged status, because, as in Apuleius' novel, it is in this asinine guise that Pinocchio's initiation will be completed. If the metamorphosis of human into animal is consubstantial with the fairy tale, if there is not a fable without an exchange of roles between the beast and the human, it is to the donkey that it here falls to verify this law at once poetic and cosmological. Pinocchio is a donkey from the very beginning and only by becoming materially such, by watching himself excessively grow ears—which he didn't have!—can he bring his adventure to an end.

Pinocchio's first—and only—offence, the killing of the Talking Cricket by throwing the mallet at him, is technically an unpremeditated crime: 'Perhaps he never meant to hit him, but unluckily he caught him right on the head, so that the poor Cricket barely had breath for a "*cree-cree-cree*" before he was stuck to the wall stone dead' (chap. 4). A mishap, in a certain sense, that restores the Cricket to his animal cry, in such a way that the brief dialogue between the two creatures that according to nature could not talk is set between two *cree-cree-cree*s. If, in the fairy tale, there is also an exchange of voice and language, if the bewitched human being falls silent, then nature, become fairy, instead takes the word, but does not forget its ancient animal voice.

In the encounter with the Talking Cricket, there occurs a circumstance that seems to stubbornly escape the attention of readers, beginning with the parallel glossator. The Cricket—in this he is indeed a 'pedagogue', as Manganelli calls him (2002: 34)—constantly addresses himself to the puppet as if he were a boy, accepting Geppetto's paternalistic pretence: 'Woe betide those children who rebel against their parents' (chap. 4). It is not that he does not know, as he says immediately before being squashed on the wall, that Pinocchio is a puppet: and yet it appears natural to him that this 'wooden head' must go to school or, at least, learn a trade. This exchange between the puppet and the human had in truth appeared just as surreptitiously in Geppetto's inexplicable change towards his creature. As he straightforwardly says to Maestro Cherry, in the beginning his plan was only to make himself 'a fine wooden puppet, a wonderful puppet, that would be able to dance and fence and do somersaults. I'm going to see the world with my puppet; it'll earn me a crust and glass of wine' (chap. 2). How then to explain the fact that, once Pinocchio has been made, he treats him like a boy, calls him son and sells his fustian cape to buy him the alphabet book and send him to school? And not only that: for the instrument that was to serve to get him a piece of bread, he unhesitatingly sacrifices the three pears that were to serve him as breakfast. Like the Talking Cricket, he has not forgotten that he is dealing with a puppet whom he hoped to 'make good' (chap. 3)—nonetheless he continues to treat him as if he were a boy, to demand of this piece of wood incongruous, all too human services.

It is necessary to think through this misunderstanding between the human and the puppet, because what is in question is perhaps one of the structures of the book that has remained hidden—even if without subterfuge. It is as if the human could truly appear only in what is not human: in a wooden puppet and not in a Christian in flesh and blood. For this reason—because only the inhuman is truly human—everyone treats Pinocchio as if he were already the boy that he will wind up being; but for the same reason, the puppet rebels with all his strength against this ill-omened fate, this fraudulent metaphysics. He does not want to be a boy, he does not want his wooden and sylvan nature to be misrecognized in that way. One thus understands why when he discovers the existence of the Great Puppet Theatre, the 'fever of curiosity' comes over him and, 'losing all reserve', he sells the alphabet book for four pennies (chap. 9). After his two infernal mishaps in the hostile abodes of men, he is finally at home, he can verify his rescinded identity.

The parallel glossator notes that the Cricket is the first talking animal that we encounter in the book. It is well known that this, the fact that animals talk, is the rule in fairy tales—a first, brief hint of the magic that invades and runs through all its most secret corners, in palaces as in hovels, in forests as in ponds and rivers. In this book as well the animals talk, but not as in the fairy tales of Perrault that Collodi had translated six years before beginning to write his masterwork: they speak, rather, with absolute naturalness, as in the *mythoi* of Aesop, which we in fact call 'fables' to distinguish them from the fairy tales and *Märchen* that we tell to children. Indeed, there reigns in the story of the puppet the most absolute absence of magic. No spells, no enchanted seeds and little animals that perform unexpected miracles to save princes and princesses from ogres and evil fairies. If Pinocchio is transformed into a donkey, it is not, as in fairy tales, by incantation or sorcery, but, as the Talking Cricket had predicted to him, by a logical and fatal consequence of his dissolute conduct. The animals that help him—the giant Pigeon that flies him to the beach from which Geppetto embarked and the philosopher tuna that similarly takes him ashore after the escape from the belly of the Dogfish—make use solely of their natural, not so magical skill. Admittedly, there is a fairy, but it would seem that her magic is singularly limited, she is not capable of true and proper spells, perhaps because from her first appearance she manifests a singular inclination and almost complicity with death ('I am dead, too!'; chap. 15).

As the introduction advised, the story of Pinocchio is not a fairy tale, it is not a novel, it is not a fable: it is a singular hybridization of these three genres, a sort of chimera, with the face of a fable, the body of a novel, and a long fairy-tale tail.

We can rush through the chapters that precede the discovery of the Great Theatre. Hunger drives Pinocchio to approach the hearth with the boiling pot, only then to notice what the reader already knew, namely that it was only a *trompe-l'oeil* that someone—perhaps Geppetto himself, as the glossator suggests—painted on the wall (but Collodi does not say this in any way). The strangeness of a poor hovel being frescoed is matched by the banality of the subject, which contrasts with the paintings which, in the fairy tales translated by Collodi, depict 'all manner of birds, fish, animals, with trees and fruits and plants of the earth, reefs, rarities, and shells of the sea, the sun, the moon, the stars and the portraits of the kings and sovereigns who reigned in the world' (Collodi 1903: 164). 'Platonic' though Geppetto's house may be, as the commentator insinuates (Manganelli 2002: 28), it remains a 'basement room' (chap. 3), and it is of this room that the famished Pinocchio searches every nook and cranny to find 'even a bit of dry bread, a little crust, a bone left by the dog, a spot of mouldy polenta, a fish bone, a cherry stone, in other words, something to chew' (chap. 5). The hen's egg that he finds in the rubbish heap—even though, in the esoteric tradition collected by Bachofen (1856), it is a mystery symbol, *mundi simulacrum* [likeness of the world] and *archē geneseos*, principle of generation—shows itself, like the boiling pot, to be a trick, because as soon as Pinocchio cracks its shell, he lets out 'a chick all chirpy and courteous' who, before flying away, makes a deep bow to him and thanks him for having saved him the trouble of breaking his shell. The second animal that the puppet encounters is the contrary to the pedagogical Cricket: he even calls him 'Mr Pinocchio' (again the exchange with the human) and salutes him ceremoniously: 'Very many thanks, Mr Pinocchio, for having saved me the trouble of breaking my

shell! *Au revoir*, keep well and all good wishes to your house!'
(chap. 5). If the egg is truly an allegory of generation and
regeneration, Pinocchio thus succeeds, as hierophant, in doing
for the chick what he cannot and does not want to do for
himself: to be born and transform.

The following expedition to the nearby village, which is
in reality a 'land of the dead', where one of the latter, a 'little
old man', when asked for a piece of bread, orders him to hold
out his hat and waters him with a bucket of water 'as if he was
a pot of dried-up geraniums' (chap. 6), does nothing but confirm the hostility of humans. (For readers interested in philology, in the *Giornale per i bambini* and in the Paggi edition—and
in the one that Manganelli reads—Pinocchio, at the little old
man's request, takes off a 'little hat', which he takes from who
knows where, because only later will Geppetto make one for
him out of bread crumbs; the Bemporad edition corrects this
oversight and explains that Pinocchio, 'who did not yet have
a hat' was limited to drawing closer under the window to feel
the water unexpectedly rain down on him.)

When he published *The Adventures of a Puppet* in a single volume, Collodi was no longer young, he was 57 years old. A caricature from 1875 shows him prematurely aged, almost bald, with moustache, beard and long muttonchops, all completely grey. He would die seven years after the publication of *Pinocchio*, when he had hardly begun to savour the fruits of his unexpected fame. It is perhaps for this reason that Pinocchio's story is teeming with 'old men', 'little old men' and 'old women', who pop up who knows how, without the author in any way motivating their presence (the stereotypical formula is: 'an old man appeared', 'he asked a little old man', 'the old woman said'). A final registry of the characters who appear in the book is, from this point of view, instructive. If not old, Maestro Cheery and Geppetto, both with wigs, one grey and one yellow (like polenta), are also, at their first appearance, at least elderly. But when Pinocchio finds his father in the stomach of the Dogfish at the end, the latter is by that time 'a little old man who was completely white, as if he were made of snow or whipped cream' (chap. 35). Also decrepit is the Talking Cricket, who, unasked, gives all his personal information: 'I have lived in this room for more than a hundred years' (chap. 4). The fact is that senescence and old age are consubstantial with the fairy tale and, in his translations of Perrault and Madame d'Aulnoy, Collodi had encountered an enormous number of old women (an old witch and a lovely fairy are, from this point of view, indiscernible), like the 'decrepit old woman, uglier than sin' (Collodi 1903: 169) who plays such an important role in the stupendous 'White Cat'.

There are also very many young boys in the story of the puppet, but—with the sole exception of Lucignolo and the 'small boy from the village' (chap. 9) whom Pinocchio asks for information about the Grand Puppet Theatre—they are not individuals, but always jumbled hooligans and rabble, 'piled up on top of each other like so many anchovies in brine', like the 'little boys' who fill the wagon that will carry them into the Land of Toys (chap. 31). The other exception is the 'beautiful little girl' with blue hair (chap. 15)—who will show herself to

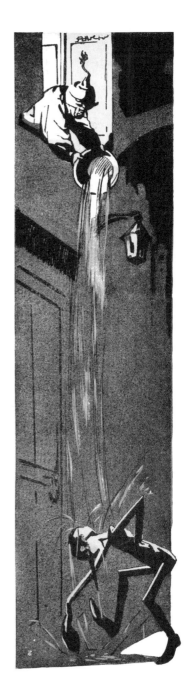

be a fairy, and fairies, as is well known, have no age: as soon as we meet her, she is in any case already dead. Pinocchio, for his part, has no age, he speaks before being born and needs only stretch his legs to begin to run and flee. But if we want to document at all costs as much of his personal information as possible, at a rough estimate he should not be older than three years when he finishes being a puppet and is transformed into a boy.

Having returned home 'wet as a drowned duck', Pinocchio, exhausted, falls asleep after putting his 'soaked and muddy' feet on a brazier full of glowing embers (chap. 6). When the voice of Geppetto, released from prison, awakens him, he does not notice that his feet have been entirely burnt up and, jumping down from the stool to go open the door, he falls 'flat on his face on the floor' (chap. 7). Manganelli comments at length on this fatal apparition of fire in the life of the puppet. The puppet has in common with plants 'the fear of a danger by turns sudden and piercing: fire'. Up to that moment, 'the fire pursuing Pinocchio has only been talked about: stoves, fire-places, boiling pots', but when, 'soaked and exhausted', he falls into his first earthly sleep, 'the insidious fire hurts him, "little by little" [chap. 6], for the first time' (Manganelli 2002: 42).

Why in the world does the puppet not notice that his feet catch fire and 'burn up' to the point of becoming ashes (chap. 6)? Certainly sleep, in the Greek tradition, was assimilated to the 'lesser mysteries' through which future initiates purify themselves before approaching the Greater Mysteries—but there is no sleep deep enough to be able to anaesthetize a body prey to flames.

The fact is, under circumstances that tend to stubbornly escape readers, while in Maestro Cherry's workshop he is

sensitive to the strikes of the axe and the tickling of the planing, when Geppetto carves and slowly shapes with his tools
'the chin, and then the neck, and then the shoulders, the
stomach, the arms and the hands' (chap. 3), Pinocchio not only
does not lament but never stops joking and laughing. His
puppet body parts, like the glorious body of the blessed, have
become for some reason (about which, as always, Collodi
remains silent) absolutely impassible.

In order to get his feet back, the puppet yields to the
demands of his father, who continues to call him a child ('All
children make those promises, when they want something'), and,
while insinuating a difference, denies his puppet nature: 'But I'm
not like other children! I'm good, much more than others.'
The tailoring of the new feet, which are 'agile, slender and
vigorous, as if modelled by an artist of genius' (chap. 8) fore-
shadow Pinocchio's investiture with clothing—an important
moment in his initiatory itinerary, if one recalls the importance
that theologians attach to the *tunicae pelliceae* [garments of skin]
with which the Lord clothes our first parents when he expels
them from the Garden of delights.[2] And, thus harangued and

---

2 Considerations on the *tunicae pelliceae* [garments of skin] with which God
clothed Adam and Eve when expelling them from the earthly paradise can
be read in Agamben 2011.

confused, Pinocchio, 'with his fine new alphabet book under his arm', seeking to give a meaning to his diligent de-living [*disvivere*], leaves home and turns down the street that was to lead him to school.

It is at this point that the encounter with the Great Puppet Theatre marks for Pinocchio his liberation from the world of humans and, beyond scruples and hesitations, the possibility of finding again his true, wooden identity. As soon as the poster that announces it is read for him, Pinocchio sells the alphabet book for four pence and enters unhesitatingly into the comedy that, as he is told, is 'starting now' (chap. 9).

For Pinocchio, the decisive event in the Great Theatre—enough to cause a 'near revolution'—is that he is unexpectedly recognized by Harlequin and Pulcinella, who acknowledge him as a 'brother'—which is to say, incorrigibly as a puppet. 'Gods in heaven!' cries Harlequin, immediately supported by Pulcinella, 'Do I dream or do I wake? Yet over yonder that is surely Pinocchio!' 'Yes, it's Pinocchio! It's our brother Pinocchio!' shout all the puppets in chorus, 'leaping out from the wings' (chap. 10).

The unconditional, comic recognition—for which Collodi furnishes no explanation whatsoever—gives the lie to Geppetto's pretence of having given a name to his presumed son. The puppets knew that name from time immemorial, and no one could have taught them, least of all Geppetto. Pinocchio is not a boy or a son: he is their 'wooden brother', he belongs to their people, and as such he is warmly welcomed with 'bear hugs', 'friendly pinches', and 'slaps on the back' (chap. 10). Like Harlequin, like Pulcinella, Pinocchio is eternal, as eternal as his people: if in Maestro Cherry's workshop he speaks and feels even before being formed, it is because he pre-existed his creation, which therefore reveals itself to be simulated and apparent.

And Mangiafuoco (Fire-Eater), the puppet-master who is necessarily a good judge of these things, also recognizes him as a puppet: 'Fetch me that puppet. [. . .] It looks to me as if he's a puppet made of very dry wood, and I'm sure that when I throw him on the fire he'll give a lovely, bright flame for the roast' (chap. 10).

What is a puppet? Contrary to the quibbling of contemporary pedants, it is necessary to recall that, when Collodi wrote, puppet [*burattino*] and marionette [*marionetta*] were perfectly synonymous: 'That wooden or rag doll,' attests the sensible Tommaseo dictionary under the heading *burattino*, 'with many of which the puppeteer represents comedies and farces, making them move by way of strings and speaking for them'.

The assimilation of the human being to a marionette is a recurring Platonic theme. 'Let's imagine,' writes the philosopher in the *Laws* (644d),

> that each of us living beings is a marvellous puppet of the gods. Whether we have been constructed to serve as their plaything, or for some serious reason, is something beyond our ken, but what we certainly do know is this: we have these emotions in us, which act like

cords or strings and tug us about and make us perform mutually opposed actions.

The term that we have translated as 'marvellous puppet' is *thauma* (etymologically linked to *thaumazein*, 'to marvel') and it is not impossible that the designation of Pinocchio as a 'marvellous puppet' contains an echo of Plato's text (the Italian translation that I have before me, perhaps like one Collodi could have read, renders *thauma* as 'marvellous device' [*congegno meraviglioso*]). It is necessary also to recall the explanation that Plato adds for his 'myth': 'the fable that represents us as puppets will have been well understood if the meaning of "self-superior" or "self-inferior" for each being is made more clear' (645b). Pinocchio will thus be a paradigm of the human condition, because—even if it is not clear who is to hold the strings that make him move and whether there truly are these strings—he is condemned, as his adventures eloquently show, to be always inferior and superior to himself, never to reach a secure identity.

Another fable, which this time Collodi could less easily have known, teaches us clearly that, nevertheless, the marionette can be superior to the human. In the essay 'On the Marionette Theatre', Heinrich Kleist begins by referring to the opinion of a dancer, according to whom in his trade there is much to compare with the movements of marionettes. One must not believe, in fact, that every body part has to be governed by the puppeteer at every instant: 'Every movement, he said, will have a centre of gravity; it would suffice to direct this crucial point to the inside of the figure. The limbs that function as nothing more than a pendulum, swinging freely, will follow the movement in a mechanical way without anyone's aid' (Kleist 1972: 22). And since it is necessary that the puppeteer, to place himself at the marionette's centre of gravity, should dance in some way, one could therefore say that the line that the centre of gravity has to describe is none other than 'the path to the soul of the dancer' (23). If a mechanic—adds the didactic dancer—wanted to construct for himself a marionette according to his prescriptions, 'he could perform by means of it a dance that neither he nor any other outstanding dancer of his time, not even Vestris himself, could equal' (23). The marionette's advantage, in fact, is that it never makes affected movements, as happens to human beings of flesh and blood. Insofar as they have tasted of the tree of knowledge, they have lost their paradisiacal innocence and, with it, grace; to get it back, they would have to travel far and wide around the world looking for a back door somewhere to re-enter Eden. Only where knowledge does not exist, as in

the marionette, is it not possible to make a mistake. But precisely this is what is impossible for a human: 'only a god could
measure up to this matter, and this is the point where both
ends of the circular world would join one another' (24).

The narrator, who is starting to be convinced, recounts in
his turn that he had seen some time before a young man of
around 16 years, who, placing his foot on a stool to dry, had

done it with so much grace that, looking at himself in the mirror, it brought to his mind the gesture of the statue of the boy pulling a splinter from his foot, which they had seen together in Paris. But as he tried to verify the similarity by voluntarily repeating his gesture, not only was he no longer able to reproduce it, but the movements he made were so clumsy that it was impossible to restrain their laughter.

'Now, my excellent friend', concludes the dancer,

you are in possession of everything that is necessary to comprehend what I am saying. We can see the degree to which reflection becomes darker and weaker in the organic world, so that the grace that is there emerges all the more shining and triumphant. Just as the inter-section of two lines, seen from a given point, after passing through the infinite is unexpectedly found on the other side of that point [. . .] so grace returns after knowledge has, so to speak, crossed over the infinite, so that, at the same time, it appears most purely in that bodily structure that has no knowledge at all, or has infinite knowledge—that is, in the mechanical puppet, or in God.

Somewhat at loose ends, the narrator asks him, 'would we have to eat again of the tree of knowledge to fall back again into a state of innocence?' 'Most certainly,' replies the dancer, 'That is the last chapter of the history of the world' (Kleist 1972: 26).

It is well known that the Kleistian paradigm has enjoyed good fortune in the modern theatre: Gordon Craig, Decroux, Artaud, each in his own way, makes of it the very archetype of the stage body, the cruel and unreserved disorganization of the human body to raise the actor to the level of a super-marionette. Ubu too is a *pantin*, a puppet or marionette, and we know that his inventor, Alfred Jarry, ended up identifying with his creation and, precisely to the contrary of Pinocchio, who is always at risk of transforming into a boy, became in some way a puppet himself. But if we attempt to apply to Pinocchio the Kleistian marionette's coat of arms, not everything seems right. The puppet, at least from what the well-meaning say, is not at all superior to the boy, and certainly Pinocchio does not propose to push his knowledge to the infinite. And yet the inverse proportion between grace and knowledge, which constitutes the centre of the Kleist's axiom, also defines Collodi's puppet, with his marvellous agility and his obstinate refusal to go to school to learn anything. Even if pedagogues of every kind never stop reproaching him for his inferiority with respect to boys, he is somehow convinced of his own graceful superiority. In Kleist's essay, the dancer at a certain point evokes, among examples of the inferiority of the human body, an animal paradigm: a bear, who is able without thinking to parry all the blows that the most capable fencer attempts to inflict on him. The puppet seems to stand rather on the side of the animal, 'in which reflection becomes darker and more obscure' (Kleist 1972: 26), but grace becomes more imperious, similar to the fish that—when, in the scuffle with Pinocchio, the boys throw primers, grammars and other schoolbooks into the sea—try to eat them, but 'having tasted a page or two or the occasional frontispiece, they spat it out at once, making a sort of grimace with their mouths, as if to say, "That's not to our taste; we're used to dining on finer fare!"' (chap. 27).

The voyage that he undertakes is, however, the contrary to that suggested by Kleist: not the mystical itinerary of knowledge into the infinite, but, by sticking scrupulously to the corporeal structure of the marionette, the attempt to re-enter paradise by a secondary door. This paradise, which is—why not?—cheap and, so to speak, portable, is, as we will see, the Land of Toys, in which, as in Eden, 'every week is composed of six Thursdays and a Sunday' (chap. 30). If it is not 'the last chapter of the history of the world' (Kleist 1972: 26), here at least time has been perfectly abolished.

The Great Puppet Theatre is for Pinocchio what the Great Oklahoma Theatre is for Karl Rossmann in Kafka's *America*, which is in its own way a type of fairy tale like the book of Pinocchio, which the author could have read in an early Czech translation from the beginning of the 20th century (or, perhaps, in German). Rossmann, too, like Pinocchio with the poster, is irresistibly drawn by the advertisement for the Great Theatre, which promises him that he will finally be able to find his proper place there. And like Pinocchio with Harlequin and Pulcinella, Rossmann is recognized by the friend who takes him by the hand and announces to him: 'How lucky it is that we'll be together again!' (Kafka 2012: 199).

Among the puppets, Collodi names Harlequin and Pulcinella and, in this way, inscribes Pinocchio in an ancient Italian tradition, wrongly considered minor. The comedy that, as the boy informs him, 'is starting now' (chap. 9) is the Commedia dell'arte. Certainly Pinocchio has in common with the masks the inhumanity of the marionette, and it is not surprising that they immediately recognize him as a brother. Also in common are the agility and the 'disciplined clumsiness' of their bodies, in which, as one recalls of Scaramuccia, their feet, hands and backs are more expressive than the face of any actor. But the brotherhood ends here. Harlequin, Pulcinella, Brighella, Pantalone are, it is said, not true and proper characters, but rather types or collections of characters, and it is perhaps for this reason that they wear a mask. In the portrait of the incomparable Harlequin Tristano Martinelli held at the Hermitage Museum, he holds his mask in his hands, as if in a ceaseless dialogue with this constitutive part of his identity. Pinocchio does not have a mask, nor could he have one, and not only due to the excessive length of his nose. Despite the fact that, after the book's incredible success, countless imitations and 'Pinocchios' tried to reduce him to a type, the marvellous puppet finally remains something special—an unspeakable hybrid between the type from the Commedia dell'arte and the character of a novel. The masks of the Commedia dell'arte have already resolved once and for all the mystery of their own life and have no need of an initiation. Pinocchio, who has also cut off every relationship with the sacred and picaresquely de-lives his life, nevertheless still seeks to untangle his string, is still in search of transformations.

Manganelli has such a special relation with Mangiafuoco that he has dedicated to him one of his memorable impossible interviews. In this interview, the terrible puppet master, who with his 'beard as black as a blot of ink, so long that it reached from his chin right down to the floor' (chap. 10) is terrifying

just to look at, is defined as a 'failed Ogre' (Manganelli 2002: 67). Collodi does not say we are dealing with an ogre: he says only that he turns to Pinocchio 'with a voice like that of an ogre with a serious head cold'. But if we consider that 'his mouth was as wide as a kitchen stove' and that 'his eyes looked like two lanterns with the flame burning behind red glass' and that he has in his hand 'a thick whip, made out of snakes and foxes' tails twisted together' (chap. 10), his registration as an ogre is perfectly plausible. There remains to be explained the 'failed', so important for the commentator and, in fact, in perfect accord with the fundamental character of the book, which, as we have seen, is not really a fairy tale but, in the same sense, a 'failed fairy tale'. Thus we learn that Mangiafuoco, despite his terrifying beard, 'wasn't a bad man', and when he sees before him the puppet he wanted to throw into the fire to roast his mutton, he takes pity and, with deep emotion, 'sends forth a resounding sneeze'. 'It was as good a way as any,' Collodi informs us, 'to let people know about the softness of his heart' (chap. 11). A good-hearted ogre is certainly a failed ogre, and his failure becomes a bankruptcy when, learning of Geppetto's poverty, he gives Pinocchio the fateful five gold coins.

In a Sicilian village, I met two men everyone called the Cat and the Fox. If every detail in the story of Pinocchio, from the Red Lobster Hotel to the Land of Toys, has become a legend, this is especially true of the two scoundrels the puppet has the misfortune of meeting on the way that he had turned down to 'set out for home': 'a Fox who was lame in one leg and a Cat who was blind in both eyes' (chap. 12). The fact that their infirmities are simulated, as we soon learn (but the distracted puppet does not realize, not even when the Cat swallows in one gulp the 'poor white Blackbird', who admonishes Pinocchio not to trust them), and that they mention, as something well known, a 'Field of Miracles' inscribes the two rascals in the lineage of Victor Hugo's novel, which Collodi could not have failed to read. Everyone remembers, in *Notre-Dame de Paris*, the 'court of miracles' where rogues who pretend to be crippled to beg meet up: but the miracle here does not concern the Fox's lameness and the Cat's blindness so much as the 'five florins' that, buried in the ground and sprinkled with a little water and salt, will be converted 'overnight' into two thousand gold coins (chap. 12). The pairing of two scoundrels is not Collodi's invention: one of La Fontaine's fables describes them as two hypocritical Tartuffes with 'hairy paws' ('deux vrais Tartufs, deux archipatelins, deux francs Patte-pelus'; La

Fontaine 1903: 74) who pretend to be pilgrims and reimburse themselves for travel expenses by stealing poultry and cheese. But while in the French fable the fox, who knows a hundred tricks, must yield to the cat that has only one resource, in Collodi's book the two remain to the very end, even in calamity and 'in the most abject misery' (chap. 36), in agreement and inseparable, linked by a complicity that borders on devotion.

The parallel glossator ascribes to the Cat and the Fox a theological and religious vocation. The sowing of the florins that they propose 'appears to have an Arcadian or mystical character', as if the florins were seeds, 'true fruitful seeds of the earth', and Pinocchio is therefore rendered guilty of 'vegetal usury', of a 'hideous plundering' of mother earth from which he, as a piece of wood, came forth: 'not without reason will he later be punished, since such impiety cannot be ignored' (Manganelli 2002: 75–76). What is certain is that the *pícaro* Pinocchio instinctively loves fraud, 'the generosity of thieves, the disinterest of rogues, the devotion of counterfeiters, the solicitude of highway robbers' (76) and that 5 coins for 2,000 gold pieces definitely seems to him to be a good price. And, as *pícaro*, he cannot hold back from seizing the occasion to make himself 'a grand gentleman' and incautiously showing the two scoundrels his 'five rather nice gold coins' (chap. 12).

The Red Lobster Inn at which the three improvised and inhuman companions—two beasts and a puppet—arrive, dead tired, towards evening is a *locus classicus* of the fairy tale. The conniving host, who winks at the Fox and the Cat (also two characters with a fairy-tale genealogy) 'as if to say, "I've taken the hint and understand you

perfectly" ' (chap. 13), belongs to the same stock as the inn-keeper who, in Giambattista Basile's fairy tale also collected by the Brothers Grimm, cunningly robs Antuono of Marigiliano of the little table that he sets for himself and the donkey that craps gold coins. In any case it is he who, by waking him up two hours after the beasts have left, after a night spent dreaming of the Field of Miracles full of little trees laden with gold florins, consigns him to the nocturnal encounter with the murderers.

And it is while he is groping his way in the dark that there occurs the second encounter with the Talking Cricket, who obviously was not dead—at least if we do not take seriously his self-description, 'in a very faint voice that sounded as if it came from the other world', as a 'shade' (chap. 13), as does Manganelli, who draws from it the plausible consequence that 'Pinocchio is entering the land of the dead' (Manganelli 2002: 79). The netherworldly shade of the Cricket would therefore be nothing but the first announcement of an Avernus into which the puppet, who had begun his adventure on a 'hellish night', would only sink ever more irresistibly.

The exchange of barbs between the Cricket's shade and the puppet shrouded in darkness is entirely centred on the opposition between returning and going forward. 'Listen to my advice,' admonishes the shade, 'and go back.' 'But I want to go on,' replies Pinocchio a good four times, provoking the second ill-omened prophecy of the Cricket, after that of the puppet's asinine metamorphosis: 'May heaven protect you from the dew and the murderers' (chap. 13).

'Return or go forward': the most proper gesture of the puppet is summarized in this drastic alternative. 'Return' means fathers, fairies, Talking Crickets and teachers ('If you let them have their way,' reflects Pinocchio to himself, drafting his one authentic manifesto, 'they'd all take it upon themselves to be our fathers and our teachers: all of them, including Talking Crickets'; chap. 14). 'Go forward' instead defines the vocation of a being—a puppet—that stubbornly has to be its own mode of being. The two directions, the inauthentic and the authentic, will be in conflict for almost the entire book, until at a certain point they begin to coincide, not so much because Pinocchio has yielded to the pressures of fathers and Talking Crickets, but because, by abandoning the land and throwing himself into the sea to swim 'heedlessly [*alla ventura*]' (chap. 34), he has liberated himself for all time from the possibility of distinguishing between return and progress, between the authentic and the inauthentic.

The fact that the Cat and the Fox, instead of holding to their original swindle (which, on the other hand, they carry out some time later), decide to transform from rogues to murderers, is another of the book's unexplained reversals. It is likely that they were constrained to do it by the jeremiad of the Talking Cricket, whose prophecy would otherwise show itself to be idle. In any case, the encounter with the two 'awful black figures, all enveloped in coal sacks', the scuffle that follows over the coins that Pinocchio has hidden in his mouth, the bite that takes clean off the hand of the 'smaller assassin', which is revealed to be, instead of a hand, a cat's paw, and finally the flight and chase through the fields and vineyards, are only the prelude to another, unavoidable encounter: with death—and, first of all, with its house.

Precisely when the puppet, pursued by the murderers, is about to lose heart and give up, he sees shining bright in the distance 'amidst all the dark green of the trees [. . .] [a] cottage white as snow', which he reaches in a desperate rush. After a long, breathless knocking and a dejected 'kicking and butting

at the door with his head', Pinocchio sees appear at the window

> a beautiful little girl, with blue hair and a face white as a wax image. Her eyes were closed and her hands were crossed over her breast and, without moving her lips, she said in a faint voice that seemed to come from the other world, 'There is no one here. They are all dead.' (chap. 15)

If one recalls that the Talking Cricket's little voice also 'seemed to come from the other world' (chap. 13), the pedagogical insect could therefore be an incarnation of the fairy-girl, or at least a herald of the world of the dead, whose graveyard abode is the white, silent cottage, of which we know only that it has a door that does not open and a wide-open window that suddenly closes 'soundlessly'. When Pinocchio asks, crying, 'Please open the door yourself!,' the beautiful girl responds: 'I am dead too' and, if she is at the window, she adds somewhat unreliably, it is because she is waiting for the coffin to come and take her away (chap. 15).

The parallel glossator rightly observes of the girl with the blue hair that 'one has the impression [. . .] that the condition of death is natural and perennial for her' and that she is in fact 'the dead mistress of the dead, the moon-queen of shadows'

(Manganelli 2002: 87). In reality, in a book in which there are no kings, neither could there be queens. But neither is the girl a witch, a witch who 'has bewitched herself', as Manganelli suggests immediately after (88). In the non-fairy tale of Pinocchio, the fantastic characters are all in some way diminished and disenchanted: If Mangiafuoco is a failed ogre, the girl too will be a failed fairy—if only because, by dying or pretending to be dead, she has lost her powers. The only magical trait that she seems to have preserved, her blue hair, also loses a little of its gloss, if one recalls that it is the same colour of Maestro Cherry's nose at the height of his fear. As for the Italian word *turchino*, which indicates a dark blue, it was in those years the equivalent of the French *bleu*, and it is with this adjective that Collodi had translated, in 1875 for the publisher Paggi, the title of Madame d'Aulnoy's fairy tale 'L'oiseau bleu' [The blue bird]: 'L'uccello turchino'. The fairy-girl has blue hair [*capelli blu*], we would say today, and not indigo [*turchini*].

And her ineptitude as a fairy, even her lack of charity is confirmed by her crude *fin de non recevoir* to Pinocchio's final plea before being seized by the neck by the two murderers: 'Have mercy [*carità*] and open the door! Take pity' (chap. 15). Unless one thinks that she is truly dead—or that she is seriously committed to playing the part of the deceased and simulating, as she will subsequently, even her burial (of which the coffin that she awaits is the logical presupposition)—and cannot have eyes or ears for the poor puppet.

Thus there occurs the first death of Pinocchio, hanged by the two murderers on 'a big tree known as the Great Oak': 'He closed his eyes, opened his mouth, straightened his legs and, giving a great shudder, hung there as if frozen stiff' (chap. 15). In the *Giornale per i bambini* (n. 17, 27 October 1881), that was also the end of the story, before the pestering requests of young readers persuaded the publisher to ask Collodi to continue it. The 'Great Oak' has been identified as an oak that is found in Gragnagno, in the commune of Capannori, a centuries-old tree also called the Oak of Witches, who, according to popular traditions, loved to celebrate their Sabbaths under its branches. A further proof of the book's capacity to give birth to legends, commonplaces and even place names, just as Leopardi's poetry has generated in Racanati a 'hill of the Infinite'.

While Pinocchio dangles prosaically, hanged from the Great Oak, the girl who pretended to be dead comes once more to the window and, seeing that unfortunate creature

who 'danced a jig in the
gusts of the north wind',
carries out her first
spell, which if we think
about it is not really
a spell, because every-
one is good at clapping
their hands three times
to call a trained bird. In any
case, it is from this bird, 'a great
Hawk', that we learn the true
identity of the girl: 'What is your
command, oh gracious Fairy?'
(chap. 16).

What is a fairy? In 1691 the
Reverend Robert Kirk, a presby-
ter in the Scottish city of Aber-
foyle, who a few years earlier
had published a translation of the
Psalter into Gaelic, completed the manuscript of his treatise on
The Secret Commonwealth, 'a subject not heretofore discoursed
of by any of our authors and yet ventured on in an essay to

suppress the impudent and growing atheism of this age, and to satisfy the desire of some choice friends' (Kirk 1893: 3). The full title and subtitle clarify what this 'Secret Commonwealth' is—provided that the subject in question admits anything like clarity: *The Secret Commonwealth of Elves, Fauns, and Fairies. An Essay of the Nature and Actions of the Subterranean (and, for the most Part), Invisible People, heretofore going under the name of ELVES, FAUNES, and FAIRIES, or the like, among the Low-Country Scots, as they are described by those who have the SECOND SIGHT; and now, to occasion further Inquiry, collected and compared, by a Circumspect Inquirer residing among the Scottish-Irish in Scotland* (1).

It has been suggested that the book is a sort of 'metaphysics of the Kingdom of Fairies'; but the 'circumspection' of the author instead makes it something closer to an ethnographic treatise, which describes the usages and customs of a people who—as the first chapter, 'Of the Subterranean Inhabitants', informs us—remain underground. The ethnographer's informants are humans endowed with second sight, who, thanks to their clairvoyance, are constantly, frightfully involved with subterranean people. And from them we learn that

These *Siths*, or Fairies, they call *Sleagh Maith*, or the Good People, it would seem, to prevent the dint of their ill attempts (for the Irish use to bless all they fear harm of) and are said to be of a middle nature betwixt man and angel, as were demons thought to be of old; of intelligent studious spirits, and light changeable bodies (like those called astral), somewhat of the nature of a dense cloud, and best seen in twilight. These bodies be so pliable through the subtlety of the spirits that agitate them, that they can make them appear or disappear at pleasure. Some have bodies or vehicles so spungious, thin, and delicate, that they are fed only by sucking into some fine spiritous Liquors, that pierce like pure air and oil. (Kirk 1893: 5–6)

We learn that they live in houses 'large and fair, and (unless as some odd occasions) unperceivable by vulgar eyes . . . having for lights, continual lamps and fires, often seen without fuel to sustain them' (Kirk 1893: 12). As to their clothing and language, they assume, like certain peoples persistently in exile, 'that of the people and country under which they live: so they are seen to wear plaids and variegated garments in the Highlands of Scotland [. . .] They speak but little, and that by way of whistling, clear, not rough. The very devils conjured in any country, do answer in the language of the place' (14). Kirk seems to hold a particular sympathy for the brownies, a species of gnomes or elves, who are often known to 'bake bread, strike hammers, and do such like services [. . .] some whereof of old, before the Gospel dispelled Paganism, and in some barbarous places as yet, enter houses after all are at rest and set the kitchens in order, cleaning all the vessels' (6).

An important characteristic of the subterranean people is their absolute lack of religion, or rather their atheism: 'They are said to have aristocratic rulers and laws, but no discernible religion, love, or devotion towards God, the blessed Maker of all: they disappear whenever they hear his Name invoked, or the Name of Jesus [. . .] nor can they act aught at that time after hearing of that sacred Name' (Kirk 1893: 15–16). They are, accordingly, poor readers:'They have nothing of the Bible' (16), but only 'collected parcels for charms and counter charms' (17); and as for their 'pleasant toyish books' (16), which according to some they possess, it seems that they can read them only if'a new spirit [. . .] lighter and merrier than their own' enters them (17). They are not subject to diseases, but 'dwindle and decay at a certain period, all about one age' (17). In any case, they live much longer than humans, 'yet die at last, or at least vanish from that state' (15). One of their firmest convictions, in fact, is 'that nothing perishes, but (as the sun and year) everything goes in a circle, lesser or greater, and is renewed and refreshed in its revolutions' (15). For this reason, as Kirk does not fail to reveal, 'their bodies of congealed air are some times carried aloft, other whiles grovel in different shapes, and enter into any cranny or cleft of the earth where air enters' (6–7). At every quarter of the year they move their lodgings and then the dismayed clairvoyants can see 'their chameleon-like bodies swim in the air near the earth with bag and baggage' (7).

It is because of this 'pendulous state' (like that of the puppet's body parts according to Kleist) that fairies are perennially sad, always 'uncertain what at the last Revolution will become of them' (Kirk 1893: 18). Changeable and insubstantial creatures, like puppets according to Plato and Collodi, fairies are nevertheless the last to testify of a distant civilization that in ancient times dwelled, like we do now, not under, but above the ground: 'The print of those furrows do yet remain to be seen on the shoulders of very high hills' (7).

Andrew Lang, the folklorist who edited the 1893 edition of the *Secret Commonwealth* dedicated to R. L. Stevenson, observes at a certain point that Kirk's Fairyland 'is clearly a memory of the pre-Christian Hades' (Kirk 1893: *xxii*). Kirk informs us, in fact, that the Irish believed that 'the souls of their predecessors

[. . .] dwell [in Fairy-hills]. And for that end [. . .] a mote or mount was dedicated beside every church-yard, to receive the souls till their adjacent bodies arise, and so become as a Fairy-hill' (23). The *Secret Commonwealth* would thus be, according to Lang, 'a lingering memory of the Chthonian beings, "the Ancestors" ' (*xxiii*). And it is perhaps because of this proximity to the sphere of the dead that Fairies—from what Kirk writes—love to attend funerals, eat at funeral banquets and blend in with those who are carrying the coffin of the deceased to the tomb.

The land in which Pinocchio encounters the fairy with blue hair would therefore be a kind of pagan hell, where the shades of the dead survive, among which should be numbered both the fairy-girl and the Talking Cricket. This clever hypothesis perhaps merits a small correction: it is not a question of a pre-Christian Hades, nor of a Christian hell: the house white as snow where there are only dead people is indeed a kind of Hades or Erebus, but it is an Erebus of the land of fairies, where dwell not human beings, but elves, gnomes and fairies after that final decay and that uttermost revolution of their 'pendulous state' (Kirk 1893: 18). The story of Pinocchio thus unfolds from beginning to end 'in hell', as announced on that fateful 'night' (chap. 6): but it ends up at a certain point in the hell of the land of fairies, a sort of hell within hell, which does not compare to any knowable, theological Avernus.

We should not be surprised, then, if in Collodi's book the word 'God' never appears, that it is one of those rare books that would never end up in a *Genizah*, as they call the gloomy, sad room of the synagogue where books written in Hebrew, once unbound and worn out from use, are preserved because they might contain the name of God. This odd circumstance should suffice to deprive of any foundation the numerous Christological readings of Pinocchio, in which improvised cardinals and deacons put themselves to the test. The mention of the word 'king' at the beginning of the fable would refer intentionally to the title of king of the Jews, inscribed by Pilate above the cross; the name Geppetto [Little Joe] would be a clear diminutive of the name of Jesus' putative father; Pinocchio's intervention to save Harlequin from the flames to which Mangiafuoco has destined him, an obvious reference to Abraham's intercession in favour of Sodom; the stubbornly repeated answer to the Talking Cricket's counsel an allusion to the obstinacy with which Peter renounces Jesus; the despairing apostrophe of the hanged Pinocchio—'Oh, my dear pa! if only you were here' (chap. 15)—repeats Jesus' cry from the cross: 'My God, my God, why have you forsaken me?' (Matthew 27:46).

The chain—as interminable as philologically imprudent—can here be left in suspense. Something from sacred scripture—for instance Jonah's sojourn in the belly of the whale—could have passed into Collodi's imagination, but that has nothing to do with the most blasphemous and insipid of the theological disciplines: Christology, all the more if declined as a Pinocchiology.

Collodi did not love theology—once it occurred to him to define the tale from Genesis about original sin as 'that famous joke in one act: the wife, the husband, and . . . the serpent!' (Collodi 1990). But neither did he believe that the truth was to be found in history: 'What, in the last analysis,' he writes in one of his *Note gaie* [Cheerful notes], 'is this string of lies called, as a pleasant joke, "History"? History, if you ask me, is a tedious mythology. We do not find anything truly true other than the dates, when they're true!' (Collodi 1893: 31). Truth, on the other hand, seems to be particularly close to his heart, and it is not surprising that he places it on the side of poetry: 'Among all the possible stimulants,' says an article on the 'Nation',

I don't know of any as potent and energetic as truth, especially when it is a harsh truth. It attacks the nerves, irritates, makes you unwell, makes you dizzy, pursues you in your dreams [. . .] in order for the truth to rightly bear this name, it needs to be hard (as the poets say). (Collodi 1892: 63)

What is 'truly true' is the truth imagined by poets, like the one that Collodi stages in the adventures of the puppet, which excite readers and make them dizzy, but contain in the end something 'hard' and 'harsh'.

Freed by the hawk, who cuts with his beak the slipknot from which the puppet dangled, more dead than alive, he is then taken into the Fairy's netherworldly house in a small carriage driven by the poodle-dog Medorus, 'a splendid sky-blue carriage [. . .], all upholstered with canary-feather cushions and lined inside with whipped cream and wafers and custard [. . .], drawn by a hundred pairs of white mice'. The carriage (which, if not for the gastronomic lining, seems to have escaped from one of Perrault's fairy tales) would seem for once to be a spell of the Fairy: but, as she herself specifies, we are dealing simply with 'the finest carriage in my stables' (chap. 16), perhaps made by another magician or bought from a skilled carriage maker.

Here begins the puppet's sojourn in the fairy Hades, which is presented curiously in the medical (not magical!) terms of a therapy and a recovery. The three doctors who visit him— the Crow, the Little Owl and the Talking Cricket, the latter

also unexpectedly in diagnostic garb—confirm what we already knew, and that is that a puppet can be neither dead nor alive: 'In my belief,' pronounces the Crow, 'the puppet is quite dead; but if by some mischance he is not dead, that would be a sure sign that he is still alive.' An opinion that the bird of Minerva reverses point by point: 'In my view, the puppet is still alive; but if by some mischance he is not alive, that would be a sign that he is really dead.' The diagnosis drawn up by the third doctor, with whom the Fairy inexplicably uses the polite form ('Are you[3] not saying anything?'), is at least irritated, if not frankly hostile: 'That puppet is a first-class rascal' (chap. 16).

For once, the Talking Cricket, perhaps because he has abandoned his prophetic nature to pretend to be a doctor, is mistaken. The Fairy strokes Pinocchio's forehead and realizes that 'he was suffering from an indescribably high fever'. Abdicating once again any pretence of magic, like a good doctor she offers her wooden patient a white powder dissolved in half a glass of water, which Pinocchio, who has again found his impertinent, picaresque nature, stubbornly refuses to drink. The Fairy, by this time fallen to the level of a pharmacist, informs him that 'the fever will carry [him] to the other world in only a few hours' and asks him perfidiously if he has no fear of death. Upon the puppet's arrogant refusal ('I'm not afraid at all!'), 'the bedroom door flew open, and in came four rabbits as black as ink, carrying on their shoulders a small coffin' (chap. 17). Manganelli suitably observes that 'the word "coffin" had already appeared, and not long before, when the little girl said to the fleeing Pinocchio that she was waiting for the coffin which would take her away.' It is certainly not surprising that in this fairy tale Hades, there is 'a great traffic in children's coffins'. The rabbits as black as ink, 'diligent and silent gravediggers' of that funereal house (Manganelli 2002: 97), are from the same family of fairies that, in Kirk's treatise, love to carry the coffins of the deceased. And Pinocchio, who drinks the medicine in one gulp and, giving the lie to the Fairy who had spoken of 'a few days' (chap. 17), instantaneously recovers, shows himself to belong to the same tribe of elves who, as the

Reverend Kirk attests, 'are not subject to sore sicknesses' (Kirk 1893: 17), even if they can at times abruptly waste away: 'For, you see, wooden puppets have the privilege of falling ill rarely and of getting better speedily' (chap. 17). In any case, the recovery not only is not a work of magic, but neither is it the fruit of medical science, for which Collodi seemed to harbour the healthiest scorn.

The brief account of his adventures that Pinocchio makes at this point for the fairy ends with the notorious episode of the excessive lengthening of his nose at the puppet's every lie, on which the parallel commentator, even though at a certain point in his infernal treatise he is transformed into a nose, does not dwell. We would do well not to forget that the growth of the nose is not necessarily a symptom of lies. When the demiurge, after having made him 'wooden eyes', crafts his nose, 'no sooner was the nose carved than it began to grow: it grew and grew and grew, and in a few minutes it became a nose that never seemed to end.' The more Geppetto works to cut it back and shorten it, 'the more that impertinent nose grew longer' (chap. 3). The nose is the expression of Pinocchio's incorrigible, picaresque insolence, and only secondarily of his equally picaresque rascality. What is in question in the nose that never ends is, instead, something like a constitutive indefinition of the puppet's nature, which, like that of the inhabitants of the *Secret Commonwealth*, is 'pendulous' and in constant revolution (Kirk 1893: 18). The falsehood here is so to speak physiological, linked to his indeterminable character, to the vagueness of an existence that for this reason can only be unfailingly missed. Pinocchio's nose without end, which no longer fits through the bedroom door and risks poking the Fairy's eye, is his truth, which gives the lie to the false antinomy with which the Fairy wants to define him: lies with short legs and those with a long nose.

The truth is not an axiom fixed once and for all: it grows and shrinks 'before one's very eyes' (chap. 17) along with life, to the point of becoming ever more cumbersome and difficult for those who unreservedly adhere to it—exactly like Pinocchio's nose.

'Moved to pity' by the very cumbersome nose, the Fairy causes to enter through the window (the house of the dead has many windows) 'a thousand big birds called *Woodpeckers*' (chap. 18), who peck at the nose until they reduce it to its natural size (once again, nothing magical, only the exercise of an inborn and habitual practice). And it is at this point that the Fairy, who before had turned to the puppet 'with all the patience of a good mother' (chap. 17), betrays her sinister familial intentions, proposing to Pinocchio that they live as 'little brother' and 'little sister'. It is significant that the little brother, rather than accept the proposal, wards it off by invoking the quibble of his other presumed family: 'I'd like to stay very much . . . but what about my poor papa?' That we are dealing with a pretext is clear from the fact that when the Fairy informs him that 'Your papa has already received a message, and he'll be here before dark,' Pinocchio, to escape his false sister, quickly leaves the house, asserting, 'if it's alright with you', that he wants to go— not to his father, of course, but according to his most secret, unacknowledged hopes, to the two beloved travelling companions, the Cat and the Fox, with whom he meets up 'almost in front of the Great Oak', precisely where the two sombre murderers had hanged him. And when the Fox—it can only be him, even if Collodi does not specify—reminds him of the proposal to bury his florins in the Field of Miracles, to make them 'become a thousand or two by tomorrow', the puppet does not take long to ditch the good Fairy, old Geppetto and the warnings of the Talking Puppet: 'Let's set off then; I'm coming with you' (chap. 18).

If one is to judge from the puppet's misadventures, Collodi is an anarchist rather than a Freemason. The Cat and the Fox—perhaps this is the reason why they are capitalized—are two inseparable aspects of the power that governs us: brutal violence and fraud, the cop's billy club and the ceremonious tricks of heads of state and parliaments. 'Simple ferocity' and 'ironic cruelty', 'the soul of the "killer"'[4] and 'the labyrinth of words', as the parallel commentator glosses it (Manganelli 2002: 107). And an allegory of the city of men is the 'pedagogical and hallucinatory' city of Catchfools (107), a sort of 'reverse Utopia' (108) where the two knaves lead Pinocchio, without any reason other than showing Pinocchio, 'in a maximally instructive tourist detour' (107), what he nevertheless does not

---

4 English in the original: 'l'anima di killer'. [Trans.]

manage to see: that on the one side stand mangy dogs yawning
with hunger, fleeced lambs trembling with cold, poultry
relieved of both comb and wattles, butterflies that have sold
their wings, and on the other, 'in the midst of this crowd of
poor beggars and the poor', noble carriages carrying foxes and
birds of prey. The Field of Miracles, on which Collodi does
not spend a word, except to say that it is 'a lonely field which

looked very much like any other field' (chap. 18), is immediately outside the walls of the city, as is fitting for a place of cheating and swindling, where the foolish and poor are fleeced out of their scarce possessions by the crafty and the rich. And it is there that one of these poor fools digs a hole, puts the four gold coins in it and, after having covered the grave with a little bit of earth, sprinkles it with water drawn from the pond with a shoe.

Twenty minutes later, when Pinocchio returns from the city to gather the fruits of his sowing, the one to make him understand that he is too 'lacking in salt'[5] and has been 'trapped by those more cunning' is once more an animal, not an insect this time, but a parrot, who mocks those foolish barn owls (again, even if metaphorically, an animal, a nocturnal bird) who believe that 'money can be sowed and reaped in the fields, like you sow beans and pumpkins'. The parrot's warning throws him into the saddest of passions, in which up till then he had

---

5 '*dolce di sale*'. In the note to his translation of the passage, Perella explains, 'The exquisitely humorous Italian expression literally means "sweet as far as salt is concerned", which is to say not salty enough. First applied to culinary matters, its use came to include the figurative sense of salt as wisdom, as in the present case' (Collodi 1986: 485n42). [Trans.]

never fallen: despair, the passion that—according to a fanciful medieval etymology—lacks feet (Latin *pedes*) to walk on the way of goodness. And it is in despair that Pinocchio decides on the gravest of his blunders: to have recourse to the tribunal of Catchfools, 'to denounce the two ruffians who had robbed him'. The reverse legal procedure or retrocedure that follows is perhaps the most subversive invention of the anarchic Collodi. The Judge, 'an aged great ape who was respected for his advanced years, for his white beard, and especially for his gold-rimmed spectacles, without lenses, which he was obliged to wear continually as a result of an inflammation of the eyes which had been troubling him for many years', is a fierce allegory of the justice—blind, like luck—that is exercised in human tribunals. After having listened with kindness and emotion to the account of the 'iniquitous fraud' to which the puppet had fallen victim, the Judge actually hands him over to the gendarmes—'two mastiffs dressed as gendarmes'—saying, 'This poor fellow has been robbed of four gold coins; seize him, therefore, and cast him into prison at once!' (chap. 19).

Of the four 'very long' months spent by Pinocchio in prison—perhaps a longer time than that spent on all the puppet's other adventures—we know nothing, except that they ended, as often happens in the real world, with an amnesty declared with 'great public festivities, illuminations, fireworks, horse and bicycle races' by the Emperor of Catchfools (chap. 19), to celebrate a great victory over his enemies. Catchfools does not belong to the fairy tale of Pinocchio: it is the insertion into the fable of a satirical interlude, an inverted mirror that reproduces the true image of the city of men. For this reason, in those four long months—which could also have been four years—it is as if Pinocchio had neither lived nor de-lived his life.

Set free from prison, Pinocchio runs by leaps and bounds fast as a greyhound towards the Fairy's cottage. And it is perhaps out of the same despair that led him to prison that he now yields to thoughts of his father and, leaving behind his sylvan, fairy-tale nature, he begins to slander himself: 'Could there ever be a more ungrateful and heartless boy than me?' (chap. 20).

The green Serpent that blocks his way at this point is a hallucinated materialization of his twofold self-slander ('ungrateful' I can let pass, but calling himself a 'boy' is really too much). It is precisely with this reptile 'with fiery eyes and a pointed tail which smoked like a chimney' that it is possible to measure the sloppiness of the esoteric readings of the book. The green Serpent is supposed to be nothing but a citation of

the green serpent from the eponymous fairy tale that the most anti-Pinocchioesque of writers, the state counsellor Wolfgang Goethe, inserted into his book *Conversations of German Refugees* (Zolla 1992: 431ff.). Depriving this comparison here again of any foundation is the weighty fact, as the glossator would say, that Goethe's serpent is a (Masonic) bridge that arches over the river to allow it to be crossed, while Collodi's is an obstacle that the puppet asks to 'move just a little to one side, to let [him] pass'. And it is in this vain attempt to slip past the obstacle that the puppet stumbles and, falling badly, gets stuck in the mud 'with his legs up in the air'. The fact that the sight of the puppet kicking 'upside down'—or rather 'nose-side down'?—causes the snake to literally die laughing ('laugh, laugh, laugh, he went, so that in the end, with the strain of too much laughing, a blood vessel in his chest burst'; chap. 20), shows that only by recovering his comic nature can Pinocchio free himself from the hallucinations by which he torments himself.

Yet the liberation is only momentary, because the self-slanders and feelings of guilt are incarnated again in a cousin or brother-in-law of the Talking Cricket, a firefly who reproves him for the intention—not the actual attempt—to steal two bunches of Muscat grapes he saw in the field. It is for this innocent, starving wish that Pinocchio falls into a trap set by peasants 'to catch certain fat chicken-thieving beech martens, which were the scourge of all the hen coops of the neighbourhood' (chap. 20).

The adventure that begins here (Manganelli characterizes it as 'one of his most obscure adventures [. . .] in which the diverse moral and fantasy themes of his existence mix together and contradict each other in a subtle, desperate tangle'; 2002: 117) is a presentiment of the asinine metamorphosis that awaits the puppet: the peasant who finds him puts around his neck 'a thick collar all covered in brass spikes' (chap. 21), and substitutes him for his dog Melampus, who had just died, to stand guard over the chicken coop menaced by martens. Pinocchio—as the salute of the marten attests: 'Good evening, Melampus'—becomes for all intents and purposes a dog; but, unlike his predecessor, he only pretends to accept the lopsided pact that the four martens propose to him ('Of these chickens, seven will be eaten by ourselves and one will be presented to you, on condition, naturally, that you pretend to be asleep and that you never take it into your head to bark'), and when the little thieves believe they are sure of their facts, Pinocchio truly begins to bark: 'and barking just like a watchdog, he raised his voice in a *woof-woof-woof-woof*.' The metamorphosis into a guard dog does not betray, as Pinocchio leads the peasant to

understand ('You need to know that I might be a puppet with all the faults in the world, but I'll never be guilty of standing guard for criminals or lending them a hand!'), an unforeseen, incongruous integrity. As the 'you need to know' shows, what is in question is rather the recovery of his picaresque identity and of the secret solidarity—even identification—with the dead that it implies. Rather than denounce the shameful pact that passed between Melampus and the martens, Pinocchio, 'remembering that the dog was dead, thought to himself instead, "What's the point of betraying the dead? The dead are dead and the best thing one can do is to leave them in peace!"' (chap. 22).

And it is the encounter with a dead girl that awaits Pinocchio at this point. Just freed by the peasant, the puppet—who is, as we know by now, very emphatically a dromomaniac (someone has accordingly defined him as 'an itinerant puppet')—leaps to run at breakneck speed through the fields to 'the Fairy's Cottage'. But instead of the cottage he finds a gravestone, with these painful words engraved in capitals upon it:

HERE LIES

THE GIRL WITH THE BLUE HAIR

WHO DIED OF GRIEF

HAVING BEEN ABANDONED BY HER

LITTLE BROTHER PINOCCHIO.

We are dealing with an epigraph at once truthful and mis-leading, because, if it is accurate that the little girl no longer exists, the puppet nonetheless believes that the inscription refers to the Fairy, who, as we will see, is not dead at all. Somehow Pinocchio guesses this, because not only does he ask her: 'Oh dear little Fairy, why are you dead?', but he enjoins her to come back to life: 'come back to life . . . come alive like you were before!' The fact is that the indiscernibility between the living and the dead to which the puppet is accustomed fits poorly with a gravestone, which is expected to be sempiternal (the girl actually never appears again). It is this unexpected appearance of a separate death that causes him to fall again into all-too-human thoughts, defining himself as 'little brother' and asking: 'And wherever can my father be?' Thus we learn that Pinocchio does not really have hair (because it is wooden, when he would tear it out in despair, 'he could not even have the satisfaction of thrusting his fingers into it'), but his eyes—which we know to be equally wooden—on the contrary can cry, unless he is pretending when he wipes them 'with the sleeve of his jacket' (chap. 23).

The Pigeon, 'bigger than a turkey', who calls to him from above and promises to fly him to Geppetto is a *deus ex machina* who instead leads him back to the Fairy whom he seems to

have suddenly forgotten. His true task is, however, that of putting Pinocchio in contact with the element that will play a decisive role in the second part of the book: the sea.

It does not seem to me to have been observed (in any case the parallel glossator does not note it) that the adventures of the puppet can be divided exactly into two parts, which in the Paggi edition occupy, in fact, the same number of pages—118 each. In the first, entirely earth bound, the sea never appears, but in the second, which begins with the puppet's dive 'from the tip of a high cliff', it is the sea that secretly guides the course of events. It is not necessary to be a jurist to know that the two elements define two opposed statuses in the Law. The norms that divide, assign and command on the land have no validity on the sea—the sea is, so to speak, outside the law. It is perhaps for this reason that the *pícaro* puppet dives down into it without hesitation: 'As he was entirely made of wood, Pinocchio floated easily and swam like a fish' (chap. 23). And indeed he swims all night, despite the downpour, the hail and the thunder, until, as dawn breaks, he sees a strip of land and a wave 'dashe[s] him bodily onto the sands of the beach' (chap. 24).

The long bath in his element has restored to him all his good roguery, to such a point that when, from 'a big passing fish, quietly going about its own business', he learns that Geppetto has been swallowed 'by the terrible Dogfish', instead of investigating or bewailing his death, he asks unexpectedly: 'Is he really very big, this Dogfish?' And once his curiosity is satisfied, he completely forgets his deceased father and, 'dressing fast and furiously, he turn[s] to the Dolphin and [says], "Good day, Mr Fish. So sorry to have troubled you and many thanks for your kindness." ' And having arrived, after half an hour on the road, in the 'village of the Busy Bees', where everyone works and has something to do, he hastens to declare to who knows who that this village isn't for him: 'I wasn't born to work!' And it is proof of the sincerity of his profession of faith that, though tormented by hunger, he refuses to help a 'sweating and breathless' man pull home two coal carts ('For your information, I've never been a beast of burden, and I've never pulled a cart!'; chap. 24) and a bricklayer carry a basket of mortar.

Even the most honest laziness has its moments of weakness, and Pinocchio finally helps a 'nice little woman' carry a pitcher of water, in exchange for a nice piece of cauliflower and a sweetmeat filled with cordial. The weakness is rewarded—or

punished—when after having 'not eaten, but devoured',
Pinocchio recognizes in his benefactress the Fairy with blue
hair, who after dying twice has now grown up to become
a 'little woman' who generously deals out cauliflower and
sweetmeats. At this point, Pinocchio weeps a flood of tears and,

'throwing himself onto his knees on the floor, he hugged the knees of that mysterious lady' (chap. 24). Manganelli comments that 'Pinocchio and the Fairy confront one another as the two sides of humanity' and that both 'are missing the opposite side of humanity' (Manganelli 2002: 135–36). It is clear that the two creatures cannot properly be defined as human, but they both find each other every time they, by betraying their semi-living, inhuman nature, become too human, simperingly, mawkishly human.

The little woman insolently puts herself forward as a mother ('When you left, I was a little girl, and now you have found me again, I'm a woman, so much so that I could almost be your mother') and the apostate puppet, with an unconscious lie that does not cause his nose to lengthen, confesses that 'I've been longing to have a mother like all the other boys for such a long time' (chap. 25).

It is thus that Pinocchio ends up going to the 'municipal school' (not private!). The first to recognize him as an irremediable outsider are his schoolmates, rejecting the lie of the Fairy who continues to call him 'my boy': 'You can imagine those schoolboy scamps when they saw a puppet walk into their classroom! There was such a roar of laughter that went on and on. Some played tricks on him, some stole his cap, some tugged at his jacket from behind, some tried to draw two big moustaches under his nose with ink.' And it is surely not in jest that, attesting to his true, inhuman nature, someone 'even dared to tie strings to his feet and hands, so as to make him dance'— precisely like a marionette. It is perhaps to belie this racism, through a sort of progressive and humanistic mimicry, that Pinocchio behaves in such a way as to gain 'the respect and affection of all the boys in the school' and even succeeds in making the teacher speak highly of him, 'observing him to be attentive, studious, intelligent, always first to arrive, always the last to give up to go when school was over' (chap. 26).

For someone who is condemned to be always inferior and superior to himself, the pretence cannot last long. Led astray by his 'good-for-nothing comrades', Pinocchio, instead of going to class, runs with them towards the beach—the sea again!—to see a 'Dogfish as big as a mountain' (chap. 26). The battle with 'primers, grammars, *Giannettinos* and *Minuzzolos*' (chap. 27) that follows contains an ironic self-citation of Collodi, who, some ten years before his masterwork, had published precisely a *Giannettino* and a *Minuzzolo*. While the former, which Collodi republished in 1880 under the title *Viaggio per l'Italia di Giannettino* [Giannettino's voyage through

Italy], is a sort of Baedeker, 'modestly put forth to give children a vague idea of Italy, which is their new and glorious country and which consequently they cannot know nothing about',[6] *Minuzzolo* in some way has to do with Pinocchio, because the protagonist makes fun of those who want to teach him the virtues and in the end runs away in the company of a donkey. The intrusion of the author is so discrete that the parallel commentator does not notice it, while noting helpfully that it is 'his frenetic will to redeem himself' that causes 'Pinocchio to fall into the lowest depths' (Manganelli 2002: 142). The fight

6 According to the Italian Wikipedia page for *Giannettino*, this quotation stems from a letter of Collodi's describing the project, written to his friend Guido Biagi on 4 November 1882. [Trans.]

in fact creates a victim, even a 'prone little body [*morticino*]' (which naturally is not actually dead [*morto*]), hit in the head by a *Treatise on Arithmetic*. And while the schoolboys run away frightened, Pinocchio, who, as a puppet, cannot accept the existence of a separate death, intones a lamentation that, according to De Martino's precepts, is not an inarticulate canticle, but a refutation of death: 'Eugene . . . poor Eugene! Open your eyes and look at me!' (chap. 27).

Carabinieri, as we know, always come in pairs, and they appear just in time to accuse the innocent Pinocchio of having thrown the book that has wounded the 'prone little body's' temple. When the puppet flees with the hat between his teeth, the policemen set a big mastiff on him named Alidorus (a third specimen of the canine race, a guardian of order after the servile Medorus and the corrupt Melampus) and the chase ends, providentially, in the sea: 'Once he was on the beach, the puppet gave a great leap, like a frog would have done, and landed plop in the water.' In the sea Pinocchio is in his element, while poor Alidorus, who does not know how to swim, with 'terrified eyes staring wildly', barks, howling, 'I'm drowning! I'm drowning!' Pinocchio, faithful to his hostility to death, here achieves his second salvation, after that of

Harlequin, which earns him Alidorus' gratitude. But later, while continuing to swim, he winds up 'in a swarming mass of fish of all shapes and sizes', in the net of a fisherman, who is actually a reincarnation of the 'green man' from Middle English literature and the capitals and portals of Romanesque churches (an exemplary one, at once horrid and magnificent, decorates the facade of the Church of San Pietro in Tuscania). Like the Green Knight who challenges Gawain in the Arthurian poem of the same name, 'instead of hair, on his head he had a dense bush of green grass; the skin of his body was green, his eyes were green, and green was the colour of his long, long beard reaching down to the ground' (chap. 28).

The one who saves Pinocchio from the frying pan to which the fisherman has destined him—together with the hake, the bass, the grey mullet, the sole and the anchovies, duly coated with flour—is Alidorus ('Save me, Alidorus! If you don't save me, I'm done for!'), drawn by the sharp and appetizing scent of frying, who, in order to return the favour, 'seized the floury bundle in his mouth, ran out of the cave, and vanished like lightning' (chap. 29).

The old man sunning himself at the door whom Pinocchio encounters at this point is witness to the third lengthening of his nose (the second due to lies). The self-defence of the puppet, who invents a 'family' for himself out of the blue ('a really good boy, who is devoted to his studies, obedient, fond of his father and his family') is more than justified by the calumnies related by his interlocutor: the one who threw the book at Eugene—whom we learn was not dead, but has already recovered

and returned home—is supposed to have been Pinocchio, 'a hooligan, an idler, a real daredevil'. While this reasonable lie corresponds with a growth of his nose by 'more than a hand's breadth' (chap. 29), at the lies that follow—to explain, dipped in flour as he is, 'his bizarre whiteness and his nudity' (Manganelli 2002: 152)—his nose preserves its natural size. Manganelli observes that, according to the general theory of lies pronounced by the Fairy ('there are lies with short legs and lies with a long nose', 152), this could mean that the second set of lies ('I rubbed myself along a wall which had just been whitewashed. [. . .] I met some thieves and they stripped me') would belong to the first category. For now it is a hypothesis, which the parallel commentator allows to fall aside; the fact is that Pinocchio gives the lie to the hypothesis and takes off 'towards the village' (chap. 29).

Where did this 'village' come from? When the puppet first catches sight of the fairy-girl's house, he sees it shining white in the distance 'amidst all the dark green of the trees' (chap. 15): a house in the woods, therefore, and not in a village. And yet, among the book's many contradictions, a village— indeed, a municipality with its fellow villagers and its mayor—there must be, seeing that it has a 'municipal school'. And the village will later even become a 'city', where he 'goes around making invitations' to the breakfast prepared by the Fairy to celebrate the next 'great event' of a puppet become 'a proper boy' (chap. 29).

In any case, a village exists, seeing that Pinocchio arrives there when 'night had already fallen', and he goes 'straight to the Fairy's house with his mind made up to knock on the door and get himself let in'. The appearance, after half an hour, of the Snail 'with a glowing night light on her head' at the window of the top floor (thus we learn that the house is not only in a village, but has 'four floors') contains a reflection on slowness that certainly has to do with the precipitous speed of the puppet. The Snail takes nine hours to come down from the fourth floor to the door, and to the insistent solicitations of Pinocchio ('Hurry, for pity's sake'), she responds simply: 'I'm a snail and snails are never in a hurry' (chap. 29).

Throughout the book, Pinocchio does not have short legs,[7] he goes everywhere in a hurry, 'jumping up', like a greyhound or a hare; he does not walk but 'rushes off' through the fields; when he goes with his schoolmates to see the Dogfish, he is 'ahead of the rest all the way; he seemed to have

---

7 Agamben is playing on the Italian proverb *Le bugie hanno le gambe corte*, 'Lies have short legs'—meaning that they cannot get one very far. [Trans.]

wings on his feet' (chap. 26). Why is Pinocchio in such a hurry?
Certainly it is not because he wants to become a boy. Instead,
hurriedness belongs to his indefinite nature, his constitutive
de-living, his not being, like the Snail,
only what he irreparably is. That is to
say, it is a matter of a, so to speak,
ontological property—transcendental and not a matter of
character (unless character
is also a transcendental
attribute, which is
certainly possible).
To the Snail's
axiom, the
puppet
could

rightly reply: 'I am not what I am, and for this reason I am always in a hurry.'

The parallel commentator, who, as he never tires of reminding us, has a very special relationship with food, waiters and restaurants, dwells on the false meal that the fairy-witch has sent to the famished Pinocchio: bread made of plaster, a cardboard chicken and four alabaster apricots, all served on a silver tray. Noteworthy here, with respect to the preceding chapter, is 'a protracted inversion of roles with respect to the colour white and food'.

> [Pinocchio] had been dipped in flour in order to be thrown in the oil; and, thus covered in flour, 'he appeared to have become a plaster puppet' (chap. 28). Now we have a plaster bread; in the mirror-image punishment that Pinocchio undergoes, bread, which is supposed to be made of flour, becomes a plaster mockery, just as meek, nutritious flour had degraded the puppet and prepared him to become food. (Manganelli 2002: 154)

In any case, 'whether as a result of his great misery or his great hollowness of stomach', at this point Pinocchio faints and, when he revives, he finds himself seated on a sofa with the cruel Fairy beside him, whose familiar admonition ('I have forgiven you this time as well, but woe betide if you play me another of your pranks!') presages the umpteenth provisional cancellation of the puppet's picaresque nature. Pinocchio promises to study and, 'for the whole of the remainder of the year'—even if we do not know how long this 'remainder' is— keeps his word. His 'conduct' is judged 'so commendable and satisfactory' that the Fairy, quite delighted, announces to him that 'Tomorrow, at least, your wish will be granted!' The wary 'What's that?' that Pinocchio inserts at this point says a great deal about the natural reticence that he is beginning to recover with respect to the world of fathers and mothers. And when the Fairy dispels his doubts and announces to him that he is going to cease to be a wooden puppet and become 'a proper boy', he immediately puts into action his counterplan, his 'but', as Collodi calls it (chap. 29).

If 'in the life of puppets, there is always a *but*', this is because, as Manganelli suggests, Pinocchio's obedience and wisdom are incompatible with his story and his adventures. When he behaves like a good boy, Pinocchio does not live, he has no story, nothing happens to him. Inventing a 'but' and unreservedly adhering to it is for him a question of life or death. And it is the Fairy herself, always secretly complicit with his intrigues, who prepares the way for him, by proposing to him a 'grand meal' to celebrate the 'great event' (chap. 29).

At this point, the job is done: all it takes is to ask the Fairy for 'permission to go around the city'—the village has inexplicably become a city—'inviting the guests'. Among the friends to be invited, there was fortunately 'one very dear and favourite friend, whose name was Romeo, but everyone called him by the name Lucignolo (Candlewick), because of his slender figure which was wiry, lean and scrawny, just like the new wick of a night light.' The night light, which recalls the small lamp that the Snail had on its head, testifies to the nocturnal and, at the same time, sparkling nature of the favourite friend. And the fact that he will be designated from now on by a nickname—and not his Byzantine (the Byzantines called themselves *Romei*, which is to say, Romans) and uncommon name—fits with what we learn a little later, namely that he was the laziest and most rascally boy in the whole school and that perhaps for this reason Pinocchio 'was devoted to him' (chap. 30; among Pinocchists, Alberto Cioci's *Lucignolo, l'amico di Pinocchio* [Lucignolo, Pinocchio's friend] (1932) merits special mention).

The entry of Lucignolo into Pinocchio's life marks the beginning of the most amazing and ceremonial of his adventures, the journey into the Land of Toys, which concludes with the metamorphic asinine initiation. In fact, Lucignolo is waiting for the wagon that will take them 'into that happy land'—in which the week is 'composed of six Thursdays and one Sunday' and 'the summer holidays begin on the first day of January and end on the last day of December' (chap. 30). It will not take him long to convince the puppet, who advances his scruples more and more weakly; but first, as always, Collodi inserts into the scene some premonitory signs, which completely escape the heedless puppet.

Announced by 'the sound of harness bells and a bugle call,

but so quiet and muffled that it sounded like the whisper of a mosquito' (chap. 30), Pinocchio sees moving in the distance in the dark 'without making the slightest sound', a little light, which reveals itself to be a wagon [*carro*] with its wheels 'wrapped in tow and rags' and pulled by 'twelve pairs of donkeys [. . .], some grey, others white, others speckled pepper and salt style, and yet others striped with big bands of yellow and blue'. The grey, yellow and blue evoke—as Manganelli notices, but not Pinocchio—Maestro Cherry and Polendina's wigs and the fairy-girl's hair; nor does the puppet take notice of the fact that the donkeys have 'on their feet' (!), instead of iron shoes, 'men's ankle boots made of white leather'. There is, in this swaddled, nocturnal silence, a presentiment, at once mystagogical and misleading, of the fate that awaits him. But the hierophantic wagon driver shows himself to be most disquieting of all: 'a little man who was wider than he was tall, as soft and unctuous as a pat of butter, with a little red-apple face, an ever-smiling little mouth, and a sweet gentle voice, like that of a cat winning over the tender-hearted mistress of the house' (chap. 31).

The chariot [*carro*]—the *merkabah*—in Jewish mysticism is the symbol of the loftiest ecstatic vision, whose mysteries must be known 'neither by three, nor by two, nor by one'; but here the two companions, who are travelling to a utopian, happy Kingdom ('a real Cockaigne', Lucignolo lets slip; chap. 30), do not pay attention to the disquieting clues that should dissuade them. When Pinocchio tries to jump on the back of one of the donkeys, this latter, 'turning unexpectedly, nuzzle[s] him roughly in the stomach and send[s] him flying'. The scene is repeated immediately afterwards, but each time the little butter man, revealing his true, ogre-ish nature, bites off half of one of the donkey's ears. And when Pinocchio finally succeeds in mounting him, he seems to hear 'a subdued voice that was barely intelligible', which repeats the Talking Cricket's rebukes: 'Poor simpleton! You wanted to have your way, but you'll regret it!' And a little later, like the divine horses of Achilles who bewail the death of Patroclus, the donkey begins to cry inconsolably, 'just like a boy' (chap. 31).

The Land of Toys, where the fateful wagon arrives at daybreak, is, as the name suggests, the land of play.

This country was like no other country in the world. The population was entirely made up of children. The oldest were fourteen; the youngest were just eight. In the streets there was such rejoicing, such a din, such a

screaming as to numb the brain. There were troops of urchins everywhere: some were playing at fivestones, some played at quoits and others with a ball, some were on bicycles and others rode a wooden horse;

some were playing blind man's buff, and others chased each other; some, dressed as clowns, played at fire eating; some were play acting, some were singing, some did somersaults, some amused themselves by walking on their hands with their feet in the air; some rolled hoops, some walked about dressed as generals with paper helmets and papier-mâché sabres; some of them were laughing, others shouted, others called out, others clapped their hands, others whistled, others imitating hens cackling after laying eggs. In fact there was such a pandemonium, such screeching, such a devilish uproar, that if you didn't stuff your ears with cotton wool you'd go deaf. In all the squares you could see puppet shows in tents which were thronged with children from morning till night. (chap. 31)

This invasion of play into every corner and every moment has the consequence of an acceleration and transformation of time: 'Amid all the perpetual pastimes and diverse amusements, the hours, days, and weeks went by in a flash' (chap. 31). The playful acceleration of time devours and abolishes the calendar, which, in Lucignolo's words, is reduced to six Thursdays (a day off school) and a Sunday. The odious chronology that distinguishes weekdays from holidays expands, to Pinocchio's delight, into a single, measureless festive day, in which it is no longer possible to discern days and hours.

Lucignolo's description is to be taken seriously. We know, in fact, that the creation of the calendar is the fruit of a complex series of rituals, which ethnographers and historians of religion call 'new year ceremonies'. Like the pandemonium and screeching of which Collodi speaks, these rituals were characterized by orgiastic disorder, license of every kind, and the subversion of social hierarchies, but unlike the 'devilish uproar' of the Land of Toys, they tended towards the organization of time and the fixing of the calendar. This functional relationship between rites and calendar is so close that Lévi-Strauss could write that 'rites fix the stages of the calendar, like localities do that of an itinerary. The latter furnish extension, the former duration', adding the 'the proper function of ritual is [. . .] to preserve the continuity of lived experience' (Lévi-Strauss 1975: 299).

We can therefore hypothesize, following on Lucignolo's reflections, an inverse relation between game and rite, between the Land of Toys and the chronological ordering of lived experience. Both entertain a decisive relationship with the calendar and with time, but while the rite fixes and structures the calendar, the game, by contrast, upsets and destroys it. And if the fixing of the calendar has to do with the articulation of the sacred, the game will have with this latter an exactly inverse relation, of deconstruction and emptying out.

Most of the games we know are in some way connected to the sphere of the sacred and derive from ancient ceremonies, dances, ritual battles and divinatory practices. Even the familiar game of playing ball reproduces a sacral action in which the gods fight for possession of the sun, ring around the roses was an ancient matrimonial rite, games of chance derive from oracular practices, tops and chess boards were originally divinatory instruments. Everything that pertains to games, the entire universe of toys with which Pinocchio and Lucignolo amuse themselves, once belonged to the sphere of the sacred. But the special feature of games, their incomparable magic, is that rites and sacred objects lose their religious aura, are overturned and become happily profane. As Benveniste suggests (1947), if the sacred is defined by the union of the myth that pronounces the story and the rite that reproduces it, games break this unity and leave us only one half of the sacred operation: on the one hand, myths, tales that, like the story of the puppet, abandon every pretence of ritual efficacy

and, on the other, actions that do not pretend to have any authoritative meaning. For this reason, as the parallel glossator knows, in the vicissitudes of Pinocchio one must not seek a hidden meaning nor extract doctrines and teachings that it is not proper to reveal to the uninitiated. The Land of Toys is a land whose inhabitants are occupied from morning to night celebrating rites, manipulating objects, and uttering sacred formulae, of which they have cheerfully forgotten the meaning and goal. And by means of this blessed forgetfulness, they liberate the sacred from its connection with the figures of the calendar and enter into another dimension of time, in which hours, days and weeks go by 'in a flash'. When Collodi informs us at a certain point that 'this real Cockaigne' endures for five months (chap. 31), he can do so only because he stands outside of it: neither Pinocchio nor Lucignolo can recognize it.

The Land of Toys is twice defined as *cuccagna*, the land of plenty. Whether we call it Cockaigne, *Schlaraffenland*, or *Bengodi*, whether it is situated near Florence—even if a distance of 'more than a thousand miles'[8]—in the Broth Sea, or between Vienna

---

8 *più di millanta*: a formula from Boccaccio for expressing an extremely large number. [Trans.]

and Prague, this placeless place contains, like every utopia, an irrefutable political motive. If the vines there are laden with sausages and rivers of milk flow, if the trees sprout with marzolino cheese and mortadella and when it rains it pours gravy, if people do nothing but eat macaroni in capon sauce and when it hails candied almonds fall; if, as in the Grimm fairy tale of the same name, in the time of Cockaigne, one could hang Rome and the Lateran on a silk thread and have a sword so sharp as to split a bridge in two, one must not forget that, with respect to other utopias, what is in question in this dream is a liberty that is unlimited precisely because it is macaronic and a felicity all the more unconditional for being playful and without calendrical obligations.

Toys, these at once familiar and disquieting objects, which children never stop wrecking and breaking to pieces, are testimony to this other world and this other temporality: something that belonged—*once, but now no longer*—to the sphere of the sacred and of economic profit. The fairy tale's 'once upon a time' is the open-sesame of this special experience of time, which the plaything jealously guards: nothing else—not the object of use, not the commodity, not the archival document, not the monument or the antique piece—so easily manages to emancipate itself from chronology, both the ceremonial chronology of the sacred and the no less ceremonial chronology of the economy. On condition of remembering that 'once' and 'now no longer' are contemporary, that they fully coincide in the instant of the game. Pinocchio thus has good reasons when he never stops repeating: 'what a wonderful land! . . . what a wonderful land! . . . what a wonderful land!' (chap. 30), and when he hugs Lucignolo for his magnanimity ('You're a great soul!'; chap. 31). Toys can be very small, but in the one who holds them they presuppose a soul so great that it has gotten rid of before and after, of past and future, in a 'now' that eternally extends everywhere.

Even in this uncalendared, de-almanaced world, Pinocchio must invent his 'but', he must, 'one morning'—whichever one it may be, a Thursday or a Sunday—encounter 'a rather nasty surprise' (chap. 31), which puts him in a bad mood. The five months in the land of Cockaigne culminate in the asinine metamorphosis that constitute the centre of the fable ('not life, but the fable of life', as another Tuscan writer said) of the puppet. That morning (it is no longer any 'one' whatsoever), scratching his head, he notices 'to his very great astonishment that his ears had grown by more than six inches'. Here Collodi falls into one of his habitual contradictions, because he informs us that 'from birth the puppet had tiny little ears', while we know that Geppetto had simply forgotten to carve them. The growth of his ears—differently from his nose, already long to begin with—is thus doubly miraculous, because it augments and expands something that did not exist. In any case,

Pinocchio immediately goes in search of a mirror and here we learn a detail not to be overlooked, namely, that in the Land of Toys there are no mirrors, that the inhabitants of that wonderful land without personal data and without identity cards cannot even look at themselves in the mirror to recognize themselves. To be able to look at himself, Pinocchio must fill a wash-basin with water and then he sees 'his image adorned with a magnificent pair of ass's ears' (chap. 32).

The puppet's (feigned?) despair provokes the intervention of a 'pretty little Marmot', who lived on the floor above and therefore addresses him as 'neighbour' (Manganelli rightly notes that the Land of Toys is not inhabited only by children, but that the population also includes animals, as if they took part in the game; Manganelli 2002: 169–70). We are dealing, unfortunately, once again with a kind of doctor, perhaps a spy or envoy of the Talking Cricket, who takes his pulse with his right forepaw and diagnoses him with a nasty fever, 'asinine fever', which in 'two or three hours'—by now chronology has permanently installed itself in this wonderful land—will transform him into 'a true and proper donkey, like the ones that pull carts and take the cabbages and lettuces to market'. Along with the calendar, the economy too seems to want to reassert its rights and, with it, the sphere of guilt and accusation. Like Adam caught in the act, Pinocchio seeks to excuse himself by calling into question Lucignolo's great soul: 'it's not my fault: believe me, my dear Marmot, it's all Lucignolo's fault!' (chap. 32).

Whether the despair is authentic or simulated, in any case the 'but' is short lived, if the puppet, putting a large cotton cap on his head to cover his ears (in Chiostri and Mazzanti's illustrations it is instead something like Pulcinella's *coppolone*), immediately leaves the house in search of his friend, whom he also finds 'wearing a huge cotton cap on his head, which came right down over his nose'. The asinine recognition that happens when Pinocchio and Lucignolo simultaneously take off their caps is the key to understanding the true sense of the de-living that awaits them. It is Collodi himself who emphasizes the apparent grotesqueness:

> And then a scene unfolded which might seem incredible if it wasn't true. That's to say that when Pinocchio and Lucignolo saw each other afflicted with the same disaster, instead of being ashamed and grieved, they began to make faces at each other's enormously overgrown ears and, after a thousand coarse antics, they broke into a hearty laugh. They laughed and laughed and laughed. (chap. 32)

'The tragedy of transformation,' observes the parallel commentator, 'is transformed in its turn into a joke' (Manganelli 2002: 171–72): disaster and despair here disclose the good fortune and hope that they are intended to cover (at least for Pinocchio—the fate of Lucignolo, who is a boy and not a puppet, will be different).

The complete metamorphosis that follows—when the two comrades bend to the ground on all fours and, walking

with their hands and feet, begin to walk and run around the room, while they see their arms turned into legs with hooves and their backs 'grew a covering of light grey fur speckled with black'—does not give the lie to that unrestrained laughter. Even though Collodi seeks in every way to insinuate shame and humiliation ('the worst and most humiliating moment was when they felt a tail growing behind'), the reality is certainly more jovial, since 'instead of moans and groans', the two friends 'emitted an ass's braying and, braying resoundingly, they chorused together: *Hee-haw, hee-haw, hee-haw*' (chap. 32). A cheerful and tipsy chorus, secretly assenting, as in comedies and satyr dramas—not the severe, plaintive denial of tragedy.

The butter man, 'all milk and honey'—now changed into a 'nasty little monster', who has become a 'millionaire' by selling the boys transformed into donkeys on the market—is an agent of the economy in the fairy tale. According to the parallelism between sacrality and economy that should be familiar to us, the little man is also the mystagogue who leads the puppet into his penultimate adventure. He sells Lucignolo to a peasant and in a way restores Pinocchio to his original vocation, giving him over to the director of a 'company of clowns and tight-rope performers', who intends 'to train him to jump and dance

along with the other animals in the company' (chap. 33). In Apuleius' novel (or *fabula milesia*, Milesian fable), which Collodi certainly would have had in mind, Lucius, mistakenly transformed by Photis into an ass instead of a bird, is also exhibited for money in a theatre by his latest buyer. And when he was unexpectedly changed into a donkey, precisely like

Pinocchio, he had felt 'excessively long and hairy ears growing' (*The Golden Ass* 3.24). Stolen by a band of robbers, he is later sold to a gang of bandits, devoted to theft and swindling, who pretend to be priests of the Syrian goddess and force him to carry an effigy of the divinity on his back, which is a kind of prefiguration of the initiation to Isis which concludes the novel.

There could naturally be another meaningful reason for Collodi's interest in *The Golden Ass*. Apuleius inserts into the novel, for no apparent reason, a marvellous fable, the story of Cupid and Psyche, which is in a way the archetype and seal of every known fairy tale. It is he who invented 'once upon a time there was a king' (*Erant in quadam civitate rex et regina* . . . ; 4.28), and it is he who orchestrated the motif of the evil jealous sisters and the sumptuous palace that hides an unknown spouse, and it is again he who devised the three impossible tests that the girl overcomes with the help of fairy animals. It is possible that the fairy tale, which concludes with the 'fitting' marriage of the protagonists ('Thus Psyche was married to Cupid, according to fitting rites, and, at the proper time, gave birth to a daughter, whom we call Pleasure'; 6.24), secretly refers to the novel in which it is inserted, which is also a fable, Milesian or not, and at the same time, in the sense we have seen, a mystery. Every fable, as we know, does not hide, but fantastically exposes a mystery. Pinocchio's donkey metamorphosis is, in this sense, a mystery, even if not explicitly thematized, as happens, by contrast, with Lucius, who is par excellence the ass who bears mysteries.

'The ass who bears mysteries (*Asinus portans mysteria*)' is one of the proverbs collected by Erasmus in the *Adages* published by Aldo in Venice in 1508. Despite his love for this literary genre, in his long preface he does not manage to distinguish it clearly from the fable and the riddle, with which it seems sometimes to be confused. It is perhaps for this reason that he concludes by suggesting that proverbs are similar to the Eleusinian mysteries, in which 'the highest divine things are expressed with trivial and almost ridiculous gestures' (Erasmus 2001: 13). The proverb about the ass who bears mysteries acquires, in this light, a peculiar significance, which makes it in a way the emblem or cypher of every adage and every mystery: exactly like the proverb and the mystery ceremonies, so too does the ass, a low and ridiculous animal, bear and manifest the highest things. The proverb on the ass is a proverb on the proverb and the proverb, with its consubstantial mystery, is a kind of ass.

Seeking to explain the origin and meaning of the adage, Erasmus cites a scholium to line 159 of Aristophanes' *Frogs*, in which a character exclaims: 'By God, I'm an ass who bears mysteries, but I'm not going to bear them any further!' According to the scholiast, the proverb arose from the habit of having a donkey carry everything needed for the celebration of the Eleusinian mysteries. This is appropriate, Erasmus comments, for those who labour for others and do not receive any profit, but only worries, 'like a man who carries food for others of which he is not allowed to partake himself' (Erasmus 2001: 161). At this point Erasmus cites Apuleius' novel, curiously attributing to the author himself the protagonist's asinine metamorphosis: 'It looks as though Apuleius were alluding to this when he makes himself out to be an ass carrying around (*circumferentem*) the goddess Ceres' (161). Actually, in the novel the ass into which Lucius has been transformed by an ill-omened incantation undergoes every kind of misadventure and only at the end, by means of a sequence of events to which the entire eleventh chapter of the book is dedicated, after having eaten a shrub of roses, does he reacquire human form and is initiated to the sacred mysteries of a goddess who has many names (among which are Ceres, Venus and Persephone), but is in reality Isis. What Erasmus suggests is, therefore, that during his asinine existence Lucius-Apuleius had had to do with the goddess, had in some way 'carried around' her mysteries, even if he did not derive any benefit from them. And that the one who became a donkey was not an invented character, but he himself, Apuleius of Madaurus.

One of Erasmus' sources, which he prefers not to name, is a fable by Babrius, a Greek author of the third century CE, which tells of an ass who bears on its back an effigy of Isis and who, seeing the devotees who bow down before the goddess on every side, believes that the honour is offered to him and puffs up with pride, until the man who leads him gives him a loud lash of the whip, shouting at him, 'Jackass, you are not the god, you are only carrying it (*non es Deus tu, aselle, sed Deum vehis*)' (Erasmus 2001: 161). The ass who bears mysteries not only does not derive any benefit from them, but does not even realize he is bearing them.

Pinocchio too is, in this sense, an ass who bears mysteries. Augustine, to whom we owe the title *The Golden Ass*—which in the codices is simply, as in Kafka's novel, *Metamorphosis*—informs us that those whom the magical arts have transformed into animals, as happens in Apuleius' novel, preserve their human consciousness and live at the same time as humans and as animals, and while being in everyone's eyes only pigs, donkey mares or asses, it is also as humans that they live their vicissitudes, the mystery of which they bear on their shoulders (*City of God* 18.18). In fact, as we have seen, there is a mystery only to the extent to which consciousness is doubled and it lives somnambulantly in two distinct and parallel worlds. Animal metamorphosis serves to access the divine world above and, at the same time, to remain unaware of it, because, although transformed into asses, we reason as if we were still human and do not understand the meaning of what happens to us; the ass, for his part, does not take notice of the mysterious course of human events that it bears like a goddess on its shoulders. This metamorphic doubling also furnishes the paradigm of all true reading: while reading, we identify with the book's characters—we become a donkey with Pinocchio and become idiots with Prince Mishkin—but in some part of ourselves we remain what we are and the mystery into which we are introduced remains in a way suspended in midair. We understand, then, why responding to the question, decisive in every sense, 'who bears the mysteries, the ass or the human?', will be anything but easy and the way in which we come to terms—or fail to come to terms—with this difficulty defines the rank of every reading as of every lived existence.

Two natures—the puppet and the ass—thus define the true theme of Pinocchio's story—or, at least, of its final part, beginning with the much-foretold metamorphosis. The puppet— the human?—is the mystery of the ass and the ass is the mystery of the all-too-human puppet.

GRANDE SPETTACOLO

DI

GALA

Per questa sera

AVRANNO LUOGO I SOLITI SALTI

ED ESERCIZI SORPRENDENTI

ESEGUITI DA TUTTI GLI ARTISTI

e da tutti i cavalli d'ambo i sessi della Compagnia

e più

Sarà presentato per la prima volta

il famoso

CIUCHINO PINOCCHIO

detto

LA STELLA DELLA DANZA

Il teatro sarà illuminato a giorno

In any case, once transformed into a donkey, the puppet, who has lost the use of speech and communicates by braying 'in donkey dialect', must undergo—'whether he likes it or not', and for three long disastrous months, after the five that pass in a flash in the Land of Toys—the subsequent metamorphosis into the 'Star of the Dance', who jumps through hoops and dances the waltz and the polka. It is not clear how the master can know the name Pinocchio, as the poster announces ('the famous donkey Pinocchio'); but the permanence of this personal data testifies that the nature of the puppet is still present under the asinine appearance and impedes him from appreciating the taste of hay, which, as a donkey, he must confess not to be so bad. And it is only as a puppet that Pinocchio recognizes the Fairy seated in a box, in the guise of 'a beautiful woman, who had around her throat a wide gold necklace from which there hung a huge medallion' with a portrait of the puppet on it. It is probably due to the emotion of this inauspicious recognition that the little donkey, while jumping through hoops, falls and breaks one of his back legs (Collodi writes simply 'leg',[9] as confirmation of the double nature of the being in question; chap. 33).

---

9 *gamba* as opposed to *zampa*, terms which refer, respectively, to human and animal legs. [Trans.]

The crippled donkey is sold for twenty pennies to a buyer who wants to make a drum out of his skin for his town band, and very unscrupulously, 'after putting a stone around his neck and tying one of his legs with a rope', throws him into the sea with a shove to drown him (chap. 33). The reappearance of the aqueous element congenial to him, which will never abandon him again, coincides with the resurrection of the puppet hidden under the donkey's features. As Pinocchio tells his presumed murderer—astonished to have pulled up after fifty minutes a living puppet instead of a dead donkey—when he had just fallen into the water,

> a vast shoal of fishes, believing me really to be a thoroughly dead donkey, began to eat me. [. . .] Some of them ate my ears, some ate my muzzle, some ate my neck and mane, some took the skin off my legs, some the fur from my back [. . .] when the fishes had finished eating all that ass's skin that covered me from head to toe, naturally they came to the bones . . . or rather, they came to the wood. (chap. 34)

His wooden, sylvan nature was intact under his donkey's skin, almost as if the two natures were co-living without touching.

Chiostri Carlo

GIORGIO AGAMBEN

With a new dive into the water, there begins Pinocchio's final adventure, which this time has a precedent not in pagan myth, but in the Bible. Once again the Fairy, as Manganelli observes, is the 'inexorable collaborator' with Pinocchio's destiny (Manganelli 2002: 184). While he swims heedlessly, Pinocchio sees in the middle of the sea 'a rock that looked like a white marble, and on top of the rock there was a pretty little she-goat, bleating tenderly and beckoning him'—but how?—'to come closer'. The goat's wool was 'of such a resplendent blue colour that it was very reminiscent of the hair of the beautiful Little Girl' (chap. 34), and the puppet, redoubling his efforts, cannot but swim towards the white rock (in which, as the parallel glossator suggests, one should see a metamorphosis of the white cottage where the Little Girl appears for the first time; Manganelli 2002: 182). And it is here that Pinocchio sees 'coming out of the water and coming towards him the horrible head of the sea monster, its mouth gaping like a chasm, with three rows of fangs that would have been terrifying to see even in a picture': it is the terrible, oft-mentioned Dogfish, concerning which we soon learn that 'his body is more than a kilometre long, without counting the tail'. While the she-goat, who, since the Fairy certainly knows that Pinocchio's destiny is to be swallowed by the monster, mendaciously exhorts him to hurry ('for pity's sake, hurry or you're lost!'—as if Pinocchio were not already a being of frenzy and haste on his own), the Dogfish, 'sucking in its breath, drank the poor puppet, just as it might have drunk a hen's egg' (chap. 34).

We do not know how long Pinocchio's sojourn in the belly of the Dogfish lasts, or if it is three days and three nights like that of Jonah in the whale, but the monster will not be

the one to cast him onto the shore, as the whale does when the Lord tells it to ('Then the Lord spoke to the fish, and it spewed Jonah out upon the dry land'; Jonah 2:10). In any case, Pinocchio does not pray like the prophet to the Lord his God, but, after the encounter with the philosophical Tuna ('when one is born a Tuna, it's more dignified to die in seawater than in olive oil!'; chap. 34), he sees in the distance a kind of faint glimmer and begins his long, silent, groping walk into the body of the Dogfish, splashing in 'a pool of greasy, slippery water that gave off an acrid smell' that he knows from fried fish. That he is to find Geppetto in the belly of the monster is predictable. The end of his pilgrimage in the dark black as ink is, in fact, 'a little table all laid up, with a lighted candle set on it in a green glass bottle, and sitting at the table was a little old man who was completely white, as if he were made of snow or whipped cream', who is none other than the beloved-hated little papa, who, as he will tell his 'dear Pinocchio', has remained trapped there for two years (chap. 35).

Whatever Geppetto has done to calculate that long interval, it is certain that by now there is no longer any trace of the happy eternity of the Land of Toys. The two years casually mentioned by the old man punctually record the chronology of the novel

C. Chiostri
Firenze

starting from the moment Pinocchio dove into the water for the first time to reach Geppetto. Since we know that the puppet was in the Catchfools jail for four months, in the Land of Toys for five months and working for the circus for three months, the twelve months that remain—for the sojourn on the island of the Busy Bees, for his attendance at the municipal school, for the encounter with the green fisherman, and for the other events that we have quickly run through—are not short, and they suggest adventures marked by a much slower rhythm than we seemed to imagine up to now. Pinocchio hurries, but in long, phlegmatic intervals of time.

In this case, though, the time is too short, because the provisions that Geppetto has recovered from a ship swallowed in one bite by the monster have run out ('now there's nothing left in the pantry, and this candle you see lit is the last one I have left'). Pinocchio can therefore do nothing other than promise to carry his little papa piggyback and swim him to shore. 'Without further ado they climbed up the sea monster's throat, and after arriving at the huge mouth they began to walk on tiptoe along his tongue—a tongue so wide and so long that it resembled a large garden lane' (chap. 35). The Dogfish's reverse sneeze, which instead of spurting them out like it should, catapults them back into the depths of the

monster's stomach, is another of those incongruous inventions of Collodi's, perhaps thought up to earn a couple more pages' worth of print. The fact remains—to put it briefly, seeing that we do not have to count pages—that, with the providential help of the philosophical Tuna, the two shipwreck survivors finally reach the shore.

Conversely, it is not possible not to comment on the encounter with the two beggars that happens when Pinocchio and Geppetto, leaning on his arm, have not even taken one hundred paces in search 'of a house or a cabin, where they'll be charitable enough to give us a crust of bread or some straw to sleep on'. The two 'ugly characters who were begging for alms' are in fact the Cat and the Fox. By dint of pretending to be blind, the Cat has actually become so, and the Fox, 'who had grown old and moth eaten', finally had to sell 'that most beautiful tail to a travelling peddler who bought it to use as a fly swatter'. Pinocchio, although he sought someone 'charitable enough to give a crust of bread' (chap. 36), disposes of the two invalid beggars with a series of three dull proverbs (Manganelli characterizes them as 'biting criticisms'; 2002: 194) of the 'cheaters never prosper' type (chap. 36). But in those two indomitable acolytes, who no longer have a Field of Miracles to get them back on their feet, there is something hallucinatory and heroic, almost like—the parallel glossator comments—'the posthumous dignity of a criminal who has carried out an obscurely, obscenely fatal task' (Manganelli 2002: 194), the obstinate devotion to a sad destiny that does not for that reason—and Pinocchio should be well aware of this—cease to be a destiny. Along with the two atavistic rogues, mocked by the puppet with a quick 'Farewell, masqueraders!' (chap. 36), it is the entire fairy-tale universe of evil that exits the scene forever, from the Judge of Catchfools to the green Serpent, from the little butter man to the innkeeper at the Red Lobster. But with this we bitterly realize that Pinocchio's adventures have truly reached their end, that the fable has somehow been cut in half and has nothing more to tell. Without his 'but', the puppet is no longer a puppet, indeed he threatens to transform into a boy.

And he already is one in a way, if now Collodi always calls them 'father and son', and with these words they are also defined by the owner of the 'fine hut made of straw, with a roof over it covered in tile and bricks' that they reach after another hundred paces, who is none other than the ever-resurrecting, pedagogical, ill-omened Talking Cricket. Decency prevents us from reporting in detail the wearisome string of good deeds that the ex-puppet manages to put together, starting with turning the water pump for the gardener Giangio for five months in exchange for a glass of milk 'for my poor father', alternating with evening vigils in which he improbably applies himself to reading and writing, dipping a 'straw sharpened to make a pen' into 'a little bottle full of blackberry and cherry juice'—perhaps a faded, exhausted memory of his old roguish tricks. For only one moment, before falling into his final docility, does Pinocchio seem to find himself again: when, in an undaunted celebration of his legendary existence in the Land of Toys, he encounters the donkey Lucignolo, by now at the end of his life. When the gardener, seeing him cry over the death of a donkey, enjoins him, 'Are you so upset about a donkey that's not costing you anything?', Pinocchio does not fear ridicule and unreservedly lays claim to his old friendship: 'I'll explain . . . he was a friend of mine!' (chap. 36).

The greatest farce of the converted puppet is when he trusts the 'little Snail' (one of the traits of the denatured Pinocchio is to address everyone with a mellifluous diminutive: 'my dear Cricket', 'lovely little Snail'), in order to cure the Fairy who 'lies bedridden in the hospital', with the 40 pennies with which he wanted to buy himself new clothes. After this overwhelming excellence, Pinocchio, by now thoroughly satisfied with himself, 'goes to bed and falls asleep'. And it is in a dream that the final epiphany—and, at the same time, the last farewell—of the blue-haired Fairy takes place. 'While he slept, he seemed to see the Fairy in a dream, looking lovely and smiling', who, 'after kissing him', forgives him for all his past mischievous tricks and certifies, as if with an oneiric, sham diploma, his new fully human identity: 'Children who lovingly help their parents in their hardship and their infirmity always deserve great praise and great affection.' The ridiculous plural assigns to the orphan puppet two apocryphal progenitors, neither of whom can honestly call themselves such; nevertheless, the personal data has by now been counterfeited and the story of the puppet has implacably reached its end: 'Now you must imagine for yourselves how amazed he was when, on waking, he realized that he was no longer a wooden puppet, but that instead he had become a boy like all the others.' The transformation would not be complete without 'a fine new set of clothes, a new cap and a pair of leather ankle boots' (chap. 36; how not to think of the 'men's ankle boots made of white leather' [chap. 31] on the feet of the donkeys who pulled the mystic carriage of the butter man). And, with this investiture of clothing, the economy too reaffirms its prestige and its reasons: putting his hands into his pockets, the boy finds there 'a little ivory purse'—not too little, if, instead of the forty pennies entrusted to the little Snail, it contains 'forty gold florins, all newly minted' (chap. 36).

The boy 'like all the others' now repeats the same gesture as he had carried out as a puppet in the Land of Toys to look

at his ears, which during the night had become 'two dusters made of sedge' (chap. 32):

> he went to look at himself in the mirror, and he looked like someone else. He no longer saw reflected there the usual image of a wooden marionette, but he saw the handsome reflection of an intelligent and lively young boy with dark brown hair, blue eyes, and a festive air about him that made him seem as happy as an Easter with roses.

(What can these meaningless roses be other than a memory of the cluster of roses that restore Lucius' humanity in *The Golden Ass*?)

It is not certain, however, that Pinocchio had stopped sleeping, that these portents may be nothing other than the dream of a puppet: 'In the midst of all these wonders that were following one upon the other, Pinocchio himself did not know whether he was truly awake or still dreaming with his eyes open.'

But perhaps the most ingenious invention of Collodi, the metaphysical seal that, in closing it, restores the story that has by now become trite and comforting to the enigma of the fairy tale, is revealed only at this point. When Pinocchio, 'having entered the next room', asks him where 'the old Pinocchio of wood' is hiding, Geppetto, who has again taken up his profession as a carver, replies: 'There he is over there', and points out to him,

> a big puppet propped on a chair, his head turned one way, his arms dangling loose, and his legs crossed over and bent in the middle, so that it seemed a miracle that he was still standing. Pinocchio turned to look at him; and after he had looked for a bit, he said to himself with the greatest satisfaction, 'How funny I was when I was a puppet! And how happy I am now to have become a proper boy!' (chap. 36)

Epilogue

No book ends; books are not long, they are wide. The page, as even its form reveals, is nothing but a door to the book's underlying presence, or rather to another door, which leads to yet another. To finish a book means to open the last door, so that neither this door nor the ones we have opened so far to cross its threshold will ever close, and all those that have infinitely opened, will continue to open, will open in an infinite hum of hinges. The finished, finite book is infinite, the closed book is open; every book gathers around us, all pages are one page, all doors, visible and invisible, are one single door, the door is so wide open that not only can I cross the threshold, but the door has become the threshold of itself, I penetrate the door, all doors are penetrable, open doors are not distinguished from closed doors, doors lead from door to door, nothing is closed, everything is closed, everything is open, nothing is open.

—Giorgio Manganelli (2002: 192)

The final page of the book contains an enigma, on which we would do well to reflect. The puppet has not really been transformed into a boy, but has remained—not at all hidden, rather in plain view—propped against a chair, and the novice little boy can look at it as he pleases, defining it as 'funny'. The two natures—the puppet and the human, which have crossed paths so many times in the book—remain separate and distinct, both present in a no better defined 'next room' (chap. 36), which, on closer inspection, is Geppetto's laboratory, an unexceptionable equivalent of the 'basement room' (chap. 3) in which the creation of Pinocchio happened. Perhaps the boy too, seeing that the puppet's body is still intact, is a creation of the demiurge Geppetto. Emanuele Dattilo has observed in this connection that 'where we would have expected a metamorphosis, a final transformation of the puppet into a boy [. . .] we have instead a separation, a division of natures, in which the piece of wood remains sleeping before the boy, who observes him, gratified.'[1] All the unfathomable vicissitudes of Pinocchio dissolve in the exegetical light'of this bold secession of his two natures. Manganelli, although he seems to believe that

---

1 Emanuele Dattilo's observation is in his unpublished *La materia di Pinocchio*.

Pinocchio is really dead, registers the split in his own way: 'there remains that dead and prodigious relic, the new and living will have to cohabitate with the old and dead. That metre of wood will continue to challenge him' (Manganelli 2002: 204).

Concerning Alfred Jarry, a critic has written that one of the alchemical keys to his work seems to be 'the belief, inherited from medieval science, according to which the man who manages to separate out the diverse natures tightly bound together during his existence would manage to free in himself the deepest meaning of his life' (Massat 1948: 12). In our culture, there is in fact an anthropological machine always at work that distinguishes and, at the same time, connects and closely articulates together the animal and the human, nature and historical existence. The machine defines the human by suspending and capturing within itself the irrational animal and, inversely, produces the inhuman by stubbornly circumscribing the speaking human being. That both in Aesop's fables and in fairy tales, animals talk—this easy swindle simultaneously gives the lie to the division and the necessity of articulating them together. In the fairy tale of the puppet, the conformist machine is thus continually sabotaged and obstructed, and in the respective suspension of the two natures, something for which we lack names, and which is no longer animal or human but wooden and sylvan, happily slips in to cause nature and humanity to diverge and pull apart. Between the puppet and the boy, whom diligent crickets, fathers and fairies have indefatigably sought to hold united throughout the entire book, there is actually no bond: in the 'next room' (chap. 36) they finally stand side by side in a clear, peaceful schism. The unyielding refutation of this scholastic and familial, pedagogical and 'dreadfully benevolent' connection (Manganelli 2020) is the secluded but non-esoteric theme of the book, which runs against the grain of the adventures of Pinocchio, who is stubbornly menaced by the agents, cops and thugs of the Cricket's machine. And this intransfigurable puppet who has remained propped against a chair will continue—as happens with every canonical text—his less edifying adventures in a series of apocryphal Pinocchios: as an undersea voyager in Rembadi Mongiardini's *Il Segreto di Pinocchio* [Secret of Pinocchio], as an improbable emperor in Eugenio Cherubini's *Pinocchio in Affrica*, as a car thief in the insipid *Pinocchio in automobile* by Giulio Erpianis, as an unlikely fiancé in Berni Scotti's *La promessa sposa di Pinocchio* [Pinocchio's betrothed], and switched with an unknown fleshly brother, Pinocchino, in Ettore Ghiselli's *Il Fratello di Pinocchio* [Pinocchio's brother].

To dominate and domesticate the animal, to correct and educate the puppet: this funereal and fallacious attempt defines the mechanism of the machine. It is a question of holding separate initiation and mystery, life and what we can know of it, and founding a science and a doctrine on this separation. Only if I exclude it from my life as a human being and nevertheless implicate and capture it in that life, can I know and dominate the animal that I am—the ass, in which initiation and mystery instead coincide without remainder. The fact is that we can bear the mystery of existence only if, like the donkey in Pinocchio, we are not aware of it, only if we manage to live together with a zone of non-knowledge, immemorable and very close. This zone of non-knowledge[2]— or of infancy—in which we hold ourselves in relationship with something without having knowledge and command of it, is the puppet, who for this reason becomes an ass and would blessedly bear his mystery, if humans would not continually

---

2 *ignoscenza*, a term that Agamben coined in *The Open*, where Attell translates it as 'non-knowledge or a-knowledge' (Agamben 2004: 99n3), is a nominalization the verb *ignoscere*, which means primarily 'to be ignorant of', but carries secondary connotations of 'to pardon or forgive' (I am grateful to Giorgio Agamben and Carlo Salzani for this clarification). [Trans.]

intervene with their pedagogical and mercantile tools. As long as he remains faithful to his unnaturalness, Pinocchio gives the lie to the Talking Cricket's false alternative: if he does not become a proper boy (which is to say an adult *in potentia*), he will become a jackass. If he wears, laughing, his donkey's skin, he does so provisionally and gladly, preserving intact the wooden matter of his puppet body, which the fish restore to him, devouring, without doing him any harm, his ears, his mane, the fur on his back and his tail.

Pinocchio's two natures are neither separated nor united into a new and more noble compound: they are, rather, in contact, in the sense that between them there is no possible representation. Here, the anthropological machine is stalled and deactivated and the articulation that it claimed to insert between them is broken. And this is precisely the lesson of Pinocchio: the human nature that the cricket hierarchy wished to permeate with its salvific characteristics is only a costume or a disguise that Pinocchio can take off at any moment. Like his asinine nature for its part, which is likewise a provisional and deciduous mask, which dissolves under the nibbles of the fish. The puppet is not a third nature, which pairs and connects them—it is instead only a void, an opening between them, into which there quickly slips and slides a nature neither *naturans* nor *naturata*, a perpetually unnatured and insubstantial unnaturalness, for which we lack names and will continue— until when?—to lack them.

In Heinrich Kleist's apologue, the marionette and the young man who loses the sprezzatura of his gesture when he attempts to repeat it intentionally are incompatible. The puppet, that is to say, has his equivalent not in the human, but in God, just as 'no knowledge' meets the divine 'infinite knowledge'. If, faithful to the unconsidered yet firm atheism of Pinocchio, we leave God aside to concentrate on the marionette, we can therefore reformulate the apologue *more Pinoculi*. In the Pinocchio cosmos there are three simple bodies or elements: the puppet, animals and humans. Puppets, as the Great Theatre attests, are manifold and eternal, but used for and subjected to the goals of humans, whether 'dreadfully benevolent' like Geppetto or decidedly brutal, like the green fisherman or the little butter man (we can provisionally leave out of consideration the indifferent, like the many old men and women). A special case is the 'very dear and favourite' Lucignolo, a kind of transparent *alter ego* of Pinocchio, whose 'slender figure, wiry, lean and scrawny [*allampanato*], just like the new wick of a night light' (chap. 30) testifies to a not properly human nature (*allampanato*, the Tommaseo dictionary informs us, etymologically means transparent:'since the transparent light showed from one side of the lantern to the other, hence the Latins took it as a simile to say of a lanky, *allampanato* man that he is nothing but skin and bones, dry as a lantern; I recall it being used in this way by Plautus in the *Aulularia*, speaking of a skinny lamb').

The innumerable animals are equally divided between spies and thugs for the Cricket and gracious comrades, like the Tuna and the Pigeon, not to speak of the donkey, which is the animality so intimate that it almost cannot be distinguished from the self, from the mystery that it bears modestly and without making a fuss. Another special case would be the blue-haired Fairy, who comes from the 'Secret Commonwealth' and nonetheless seems to act always and everywhere as an accomplice of the well-meaning Cricket. In truth, the fairy-girl, as testimony to the incongruous presence of the fairy tale in the chimerical novel, always belies her connivance with humans and unfailingly drives Pinocchio on into his adventurous 'buts'. A failed fairy, therefore—as failed as the ogre Mangiafuoco—whose true task is to remind readers that the book that they are glancing through is not a fairy tale, is not a novel, is not at all ascribable to any literary genre. Something similar holds for the Cat and the Fox, who—neither truly animal nor fully human—have escaped *flagranti crimine* from a book of fables.

Between these two irregular categories (category etymologically means 'accusation'), the puppet is not a substance or a person (a mask), is not a 'who' or 'what', but only a 'how': he is, in the strictest sense of the word, a way out or a line of flight—for this reason he does nothing but run, and when he finally stops he is lost.

The puppet is, in this sense, a cypher of infancy, on condition that we understand that the child not only is not an adult *in potentia*, but his status is neither a condition nor an age: it is a line of flight. From what? From all the antinomies that define our culture, between ass and human, certainly, between madness and reason, but even before that between the proper boy (who is only an immature adult) and the untamed piece of wood. Through all of life, the child—stubborn and immortal like Pinocchio—does nothing but flee from adulthood, which it encircles and accompanies without respite, giving so much trouble to psychoanalysts and educators, condemned to see it tirelessly resurface from the Acherontic depths and comfortable nurseries in which they believed they had firmly imprisoned it.

Let us cautiously attempt to reread the book's final lines. Pinocchio turns to look at the puppet propped against a chair and, 'after he had looked for a bit, he said to himself with the greatest satisfaction: "How funny I was when I was a puppet!"' (chap. 36). What is in question in this 'satisfaction [*compiacenza*]'? Is it that self-satisfaction that the Tommaseo registers as a 'sin of complacency'? Or are we not rather dealing, as the same invaluable dictionary suggests, with 'a higher satisfaction', exemplified in a quotation from Father Segneri, in whom the parallel glossator finds 'the sonority, the minatory monotone of great Baroque preaching' (Manganelli 2020)? 'How then,' says the deaf seventeenth-century Jesuit, 'can rancour find a place in my heart against someone who will for all eternity be the blessed object of my *compiacenza*?' *Compiacenza* is therefore the opposite of rancour and it is in this dry way, free of all resentment, that Pinocchio regards as 'a blessed object' the puppet with 'his arms dangling loose and his legs crossed over and bent in the middle' (chap. 36).

It is in light of this higher satisfaction that it is necessary not to let escape us, in the sentence that immediately follows, the ambiguous repetition of the imperfect 'I was [*ero*]': 'How funny I was, when I was a puppet!' (chap. 36). Despite their grammatical identity as first-person singular, the two verbs do not actually have the same subject: 'When I (the boy) *was* a puppet, how funny he (the puppet) *was*!' If we recall that the imperfect expresses a continuing and unconcluded action or state, of which one does not want to or cannot specify the beginning and end, this means, on the one hand, that between the puppet and the boy there is at once distance and promiscuity, and on the other, that the pendulous and adventurous existence of Pinocchio deserves to be defined with an adjective—funny [*buffo*]—that in Tommaseo designates 'whoever plays the pleasant part, especially in a play'. 'Hence the French,' adds the tireless lexicographer, 'at the Italian Opera [say] *aux bouffes*, and I heard Fouriel say it.' If 'a good *buffo* is more rare than a serious tenor', perhaps the final meaning of the marvellous puppet's existence is suggested in the sentence from Algarotti that immediately follows: 'To the decorum of such representations no small wrong was done by the introduction of funny characters [*personaggi buffi*], who were not closely connected with the heroes and the gods and who, with their causing people to laugh at inappropriate times, disrupted the gravity of the action.' The puppet is not connected 'with the heroes and the gods', he 'disrupts' them and does them in with his 'causing people to laugh at inappropriate times'. Once again he is a way out, from theology, from the epic and from every grave action, towards a lightness that is stripped down but quick [*svelta*], once again in the sense reported by the dictionarist: 'one says *svelta*, as if in the act of rising from the ground and climbing', and it comes perhaps 'from being the easiest form to move, almost standing out from the place where it is'.

Géza Róheim, who as an anthropologist had done his field work among Indigenous Australian people and as a psychoanalyst had been a student of Sándor Ferenczi, was especially susceptible to fairy tales. In his book *The Gates of the Dream*, after having described in detail all kinds of witches, he dedicates an entire chapter to 'The Nature of Ogres'. What is significant, however, is above all the title of this voluminous, haphazard collection of writings. The dream here is not, as in Freud, precious interpretive material for the analysis of the soul: rather, just the opposite is true, namely, that the soul is 'a concept derived from the dream' (Róheim 1952: 259).

Dreams constitute the model for all our spiritual adventures, the privileged exemplar of all—whether hellish or paradisiacal—that we manage to imagine beyond or below the real worlds. Better: dreams are themselves a reality, they are themselves a death, a katabasis and a descent into hell, and not only an image or a symbol, just as waking up is really a new birth. And fairy tales, which are nothing but the perfect equivalent of the oneiric experience, insofar as dreams are also in some way real, also watch over a *descensus Averno*.

His teacher Ferenczi, who, as is well known, had a special relationship with the sea, stubbornly maintained, even at the cost of irritating Freud, that the fundamental human impulse was the return to one's primordial existence in the depths of the ocean, of which intrauterine life was only a repetition. This explains why Róheim, forgetting the reality of the oneiric experience, persisted in considering dreams and the renunciation of the object-world as a uterine regression. But if we recall that for him dreams are not a symbolic fabulation of life, but are 'the guardian of life during sleep' (Róheim 1952: 545), are themselves still in some way life, then we can look with new eyes on the story of Pinocchio and his descent into hell.

In Collodi's chimerical fairy tale, Pinocchio falls asleep three times, once without dreaming (or at least without Collodi telling us anything about it) and twice dreaming. The first is when, on the 'hellish night', having returned home 'wet

as a drowned duck', he falls asleep propping his feet 'on a brazier full of glowing embers' (chap. 6) and, on awaking, does not realize that 'his feet were burned to bits' (chap. 7). The second is on another hellish night, at the Red Lobster Inn in the company of the two beloved rogues:

> No sooner had Pinocchio climbed into bed than he fell sound asleep and began to dream. In his dream he seemed to be in a field, and this field was full of little trees laden with bunches of fruit, and these bunches were laden with gold florins; swayed by the wind, they went *ting ting ting*, as if they wanted to say, 'whoever wishes, may come and take us'. (chap. 13)

The third time is at the end of the book, when, after having woven baskets 'until after midnight', he falls asleep in his bed and dreams of the Fairy who forgives him for his mischievous tricks; and it is upon waking up from this hypnotic dream that he realizes he is 'no longer a wooden puppet'. Collodi nonetheless takes care to specify that perhaps he has not truly woken up and that he 'did not know whether he was truly awake or still dreaming with his eyes open' (chap. 36).

If we accept the threefold equation between dream, fairy tale and life suggested by Róheim, we can honestly imagine—

all the more so since we know that Pinocchio that night 'went on sleeping and snoring' (chap. 6)—that he had actually also dreamt the first time and he had never stopped dreaming from then on (which explains why he did not realize that his feet were burning). All the adventures narrated in the book—including the final, false transfiguration—would be only a dream of the marvellous puppet, who dreams at the end of waking up and in a dream sees himself asleep 'propped against a chair' (chap. 36), precisely as at the beginning he had fallen asleep on a chair, 'propping his feet over a brazier' (chap. 6). But the dream is no less real than waking, it is only the other face of the mystery that—like the puppet, like the donkey with its 'light grey coat speckled with black' (chap. 32)—without realizing it, we continue to bear.

Works Cited

AGAMBEN, Giorgio. 2004. *The Open: Between Man and Animal* (Kevin Attell trans.). Stanford, CA: Stanford University Press.

———. 2011. *Nudities* (David Kishik and Stefan Pedatella trans). Stanford, CA: Stanford University Press.

———. 2018. *The Adventure* (Lorenzo Chiesa trans.). Boston: MIT Press.

APULEIUS. 1915. *The Golden Ass: Being the Metamorphoses of Apuleis* (William Adlington and Stephen Gaselee trans and eds). Loeb Classical Library. Cambridge, MA: Harvard University Press.

ARISTOPHANES. 1998. *Frogs, Assemblywomen, Wealth* (Jeffrey Henderson trans. and ed.). Loeb Classical Library. Cambridge, MA: Harvard University Press.

ARISTOTLE. 1952. *The Works of Aristotle: Volume 12, Select Fragments* (David Ross ed.). Oxford: Clarendon Press.

———. 1984. *The Complete Works of Aristotle: The Revised Oxford Translation*, 2 VOLS (Jonathan Barnes ed.). Princeton, NJ: Princeton University Press.

AUGUSTINE. 2003. *Concerning the City of God against the Pagans* (Henry Bettenson trans.). New York: Penguin.

BACHOFEN, J. J. 1856. *Versuch über die Gräbersymbolik der Alten*. Basel.

BENJAMIN, Walter. 1977. 'Surrealismus' in *Gesammetle Schriften*, VOL. 2, PART 1. Frankfurt: Suhrkamp. English translation: 'Surrealism: The Last Snapshot of the European Intelligentsia' in *Selected Writings, Volume 2, Part 1: 1927–1930* (Rodney Livingstone et al. trans, Michael W. Jennings, Howard Eiland and Gary Smith eds). Cambridge, MA: Belknap Press of Harvard University Press, 1999.

BENVENISTE, Émile. 1947. 'Le jeu et le sacré'. *Deucalion* 2.

CALCIDIUS. 2016. *On Plato's 'Timaeus'* (John Magee trans. and ed.). Cambridge, MA: Harvard University Press.

CALVINO, Carlo. 2007. 'Ma Collodi non esiste' in *Saggi 1945–1985*. Milan: Mondadori.

CAMPO, Cristina. 1987. *Il flauto e il tappeto* in *Gli imperdonabili*. Milan: Adelphi.

CIOCI, Alberto. 1932. *Lucignolo, l'amico di Pinocchio*. Florence: Bemporad.

COLLODI, Carlo. 1892. *Divagazioni critico-umoristiche* (Giuseppe Rigutini ed.). Florence: Bemporad.

———. 1903. *I racconti delle fate*. Florence: Bemporad.

———. 1911. *Le avventure di Pinocchio: storia di un Burattino* (Carlo Chiostri ill.). Florence: Bemporad.

———. 1948. *Tutto Collodi, per i piccoli e per i grandi* (Pietro Pancrazi ed.). Florence: Le Monnier.

———. 1893. *Note gaie*, 2ND EDN (Giuseppe Rigutini ed.). Florence: Bemporad.

——. 1983. *Le avventure di Pinocchio*. Pescia: Fondazione Nazionale C. Collodi.

——. 1986. *The Adventures of Pinocchio / Le Avventure di Pinocchio* (Nicolas J. Perella trans.). Berkeley: University of California Press.

——. 1990. *Cronache dell'ottocento* (Daniela Marcheschi ed.). Pisa: ETS.

——. 1995. *Opere* (Daniela Marcheschi ed.). Meridiani. Milan: Mondadori.

——. 2009a. *The Adventures of Pinocchio* (Ann Lawson Lucas trans.). New York: Oxford University Press.

——. 2009b. *The Adventures of Pinocchio* (Geoffrey Brock trans.). New York: New York Review Books.

——. 2010. *Un romanzo in vapore. Da Firenze a Livorno*. Pescia: Fondazione Nazionale C. Collodi.

ERASMUS, Desiderius. 2001. *The Adages of Erasmus* (William Watson Barker trans. and ed.). Toronto: University of Toronto Press.

JAKOBSON, Roland, and Pëtr Bogatryev. 1966. 'Die Folklore als eine besondere Form des Schaffens' in Roland Jackobson, *Selected Writings*, VOL. 4. Paris-The Hague: Mouton, pp. 1–15. English translation: 'Folklore as a Special Form of Creativity' in *The Prague School: Selected Writings, 1929–1946* (Peter Steiner ed.). Austin: University of Texas Press, 2014, pp. 32–46.

KAFKA, Franz. 2012. *The Man Who Disappeared (America)* (Ritchie Robertson trans.). New York: Oxford University Press.

KERÉNYI, Károly. 1927. *Die griechisch-orientalische Roman literatur in religionsgeschichtlicher Beleuchtung.* Tübingen: Mohr.

KIRK, Robert. 1893. *The Secret Commonwealth of Elves, Fauns, and Fairies* (Andrew Lang ed.). London: David Nutt.

KLEIST, Heinrich. 1972. 'On the Marionette Theatre' (Thomas G. Neumiller trans.). *The Drama Review* 16(3): 22–26.

LA FONTAINE, Jean de la. 1903. *Fifty Fables by La Fontaine* (Kenneth McKenzine ed.). New York: American Book Company.

LÉVI-STRAUSS, Claude. 1975. 'Mythe et oubli' in Julia Kristeva, Jean-Claude Milner and Nicolas Ruwet (eds), *Langue, discours, société: Pour Émile Benveniste.* Paris: Seuil.

MANGANELLI, Giorgio. 1994. *Il rumore sottile della prosa.* Milan: Adelphi.

———. 2002. *Pinocchio: Un libro parallelo.* New ed. Milan: Adelphi.

———. 2014a. *Agli dèi ulteriori.* Milan: Adelphi.

———. 2014b. *Dall'inferno.* Milan: Adelphi.

———. 2020. *Concupiscenza libraria.* Milan: Adelphi.

MARCHESCHI, Daniela. 1990. *Collodi ritrovato.* Pisa: ETS.

MARTINO, Ernesto de. 2021. *Morte e pianto rituale. Dal lamento funebre antico al pianto di Maria.* Turin: Einaudi.

MASSAT, René. 1948. Preface to Alfred Jarry, *Oeuvres completes,* VOL. 1. Lausanne and Montecarlo: Editions du Livre.

MERKELBACH, Reinhold. 1962. *Roman und Mysterium in der Antike.* Munich: Beck.

MINGE, J. P. (ed.). 1985. *Patrologiae Cursus Completus, Series Graeca*, VOL. 87. Paris.

NIETZSCHE, Friedrich. 1997. *Twilight of the Idols: Or, How to Philosophize with a Hammer* (Richard Polt trans.). Indianapolis, IN: Hackett.

ORIGEN. 1885. *De Principiis* (Frederick Crombie trans.) in *Ante-Nicene Fathers*, VOL. 4 (Alexander Roberts, James Donaldson and A. Cleveland Coxe eds). Buffalo, NY: Christian Literature Publishing. Available online (Kevin Knight ed.): https://bit.ly/3fW8hWP (last accessed: 10 November 2022).

PETIT, Françoise (ed.). 1991. *La Chaîne sur la Genèse: Chapitres 1 à 3*. Leuven: Peeters.

PHAEDRUS. 1984. *Babrius and Phaedrus* (Ben Edwin Perry trans. and ed.). Loeb Classical Library. Cambridge, MA: Harvard University Press.

PLATO. 1997. *Complete Works* (John Cooper and D. S. Hutchinson eds). Indianapolis, IN: Hackett.

RÓHEIM, Géza. 1952. *The Gates of the Dream*. New York: International Universities Press.

SIMONETTI, Manlio (ed.). 1970. *Testi gnostici cristiani*. Rome: Laterza.

TOMMASEO, Niccolò. 1865. *Dizionario della lingua Italiana*, 4VOLS. Turin: Società L'Unione Tipografico-Editrice.

ZOLLA, Elémire. 1992. *Uscite dal mondo*. Milan: Adelphi.

———. 2002. 'Il burattino framassone', interview with S. Ronchey. *La Stampa* (27 February).

A Note on Illustrations

The Italian edition of this volume is a graphic project designed by Viviana Gottardello in collaboration with the author. In this English edition, we have endeavoured to reproduce the same design to the best of our ability.

The illustrations are taken from:

C. Collodi, *Le avventure di Pinocchio. Storia di un burattino*. Illustrated by E. Mazzanti. Florence: Felice Paggi Libraio Editore, 1883. Reproduced here on pages 2, 44, 60, 86, 87, 100, 104, 116, 117, 126, 140.

C. Collodi, *Le avventure di Pinocchio. Storia di un burattino*. Illustrated by C. Chiostri. Florence: R. Bemporad e Figlio Editori, 1901. Reproduced here on pages 4, 33, 41, 49, 53, 72, 78, 83, 90, 106, 113, 119, 120, 123, 130, 133, 149, 152, 154, 160, 163, 165, 167, 169, 174.

Le avventure di Pinocchio di C. Collodi. Colour drawings by A. Mussino. Florence: R. Bemporad e Figlio Editori, 1911. Reproduced here on pages 10, 13, 22, 24, 32, 50, 54, 63, 65, 67, 81, 92, 102, 109, 128, 144–45, 177, 190, 192, 199. Illustrations reproduced with the kind permission of Giunti Editore S.p.A.